BRITAIN IN OLD PHOTOGRAPHS

HACKNEY, HOMERTON & DALSTON

Prime Bang Up at Hackney or a peep at the Balloon. Balloon trips were the thing of the moment in the first two decades of the nineteenth century, with ascents from the Mermaid Gardens on the west side of Church Street (Mare Street) and from Hackney Wick. Here, cartoonist Thomas Tegg has fun at the expense of the audience of an ascent in 1811.

BRITAIN IN OLD PHOTOGRAPHS

HACKNEY,
HOMERTON & DALSTON

PRINTS AND ENGRAVINGS 1720–1948
FROM THE COLLECTIONS AT HACKNEY ARCHIVES DEPARTMENT

DAVID MANDER

LONDON BOROUGH OF HACKNEY
SUTTON PUBLISHING LIMITED

Sutton Publishing Limited
Phoenix Mill · Thrupp · Stroud
Gloucestershire · GL5 2BU
in association with Hackney Archives Department
First published 1996

Copyright © David Mander, 1996

Cover photographs: *front:* Mare Street, the
Narrow Way, 1904; *back:* homeward bound for
Messrs Abbott's foreman on Homerton Road,
approaching Marshgate bridge, 1905.

British Library Cataloguing in Publication Data
A catalogue record for this book is available from the
British Library.

ISBN 0-7509-1228-6

Typeset in 10/12 Perpetua.
Typesetting and origination by
Sutton Publishing Limited.
Printed in Great Britain by
Ebenezer Baylis, Worcester

FOR MORGAN

ACKNOWLEDGEMENTS

The reproduction rights of all photographs in this book are vested in LB Hackney, Hackney Archives Department, with the following exceptions, who are thanked for their permission to use the images.

Akzo Nobel (pp. 139–141); Mr D. Beresford Johnson (p. 74, bottom); Mrs Josephine Boyle (p. 86–7, 88, top, 90–91); Miss Betty Brett (p. 62, bottom); Carless Refining and Marketing Ltd (p. 142); Corporation of London, Greater London Record Office (p. 52, p. 113); and Guildhall Library (p. 88, bottom, pp. 97–8, p. 113, top); Elizabeth Fry Probation and Bail Hostel (p. 101); GEC-Marconi (p. 144, top); Rear Admiral J.A.L. Myres (p. 93); Royal Commission on the Historical Monuments of England, (Crown copyright, p. 89); Mr Dick Whetstone (p. 103 top, p. 129 top).

The Author regrets that no addresses survive at Hackney Archives Department for the following, who are thanked for the use of copies of their original photographs: Ms D. Chardin (p. 145, top); Mrs Kruger (p. 64, bottom). The author would also like to thank Isobel Watson on her comments on the draft text.

If you enjoyed this book and want to be kept informed of what else is published on Hackney's history, you may be interested in the Friends of Hackney Archives, which serves as the local history society and a user group for the Archives Department.

Friends receive three newsletters a year and an annual volume of historical articles, together with details of any special offers on new books produced by the Archives Department. As the credits for this book make clear, the visual collection has been enriched by many original photographs given or loaned for copying.

If you have something that you think might interest us, please get in touch. The address for the department and for membership details about the Friends of Hackney Archives is: Hackney Archives Department, 43 De Beauvoir Road, London N1 5SQ. Tel. (0)171 241 2886. Fax (0)171 241 6688. E-mail: archives@hackney.gov.uk.

The department is not open every day. Please phone for details and an appointment.

CONTENTS

Midwinter in Hackney Churchyard, *c.* 1885. Alfred Braddock braved the snow to include the Old Church Tower, a symbol of Hackney, and the churchyard in this photograph. The squat building is the Rowe Chapel – actually a mausoleum built for the Rowe family, then lords of the manor, in 1614, which was demolished after it had become unsafe, before 1913. This part of the churchyard was cleared of the majority of tombstones in 1893–4, though not without criticism in the press.

INTRODUCTION

Welcome to the third selection of old photographs from the collection of the London Borough of Hackney's Archives Department, and the fifth Hackney photographic work I have been involved in since 1989. A previous volume, *Stoke Newington, Stamford Hill and Upper Clapton in Old Photographs*, covered the northern part of the borough. *More Light, More Power: An Illustrated History of Shoreditch*, published this year, covered the old metropolitan borough of Shoreditch. The present book covers the bits of Hackney in the middle, and rather more than the title implies.

Firstly, there are more places than the three in the title. 'Hackney' includes South Hackney, the isolated Hackney Wick and a glance at Hackney Marshes. 'Dalston' includes the modern Dalston (actually the old Kingsland), Shacklewell (a lost Hackney village if ever there was one) and De Beauvoir Town.

Secondly, I have included views copied from engravings, watercolours, lithographs and other non-photographic sources. This has allowed me to cover a greater range in time. Hackney was not a static community in the 1860s, when photography was beginning to gain popularity, and although change accelerated in the late nineteenth century, many buildings and scenes had already been lost forever, or were not photographed while there was time to do so. It was left to artists to capture the brickfields that provided the fabric of Victorian Hackney, the farms and country lanes, and much else besides.

Hackney is lucky in that the Tyssen family, the largest of Hackney estate owners and lords of the principal manors, also took an interest in the history of the area. In the early nineteenth century they commissioned artists and architects to draw buildings that were threatened by development, and bought up drawings and watercolours from the estate of artists like T. Fisher and George Hawkins. Hawkins had produced his own prints for sale, but also left behind a mass of watercolours and sketches at his death, almost all of which seem to have been acquired by the Tyssens. Their books, documents and drawings, housed in the second Hackney Town Hall from the 1880s, passed to the newly created Hackney Public Library in 1908 and form the principal nucleus of Hackney Archives Department's collections today.

In my first selection of old photographs, I drew on the works of two local photographers, George James, operating from the mid-1860s to around 1875, and Alfred Braddock, who was active from the late 1870s to around 1910. Both of these men feature again in this book. I have a special fondness for James's work. He would have made most of his money from portrait photography, where the subject came to the camera. Lugging bulky equipment out on to the street must have been a laborious business, even if he hoped to profit by selling his small, mounted *carte de visite* prints locally. If James is identical with the George James working from 130 Euston Road from 1875, it would explain why we appear to have no later examples of his work. However Braddock, who produced postcard-sized prints, also mounted on card, was a worthy successor, and benefited from the improvements in equipment and developing from the mid-1870s onwards.

This book is arranged geographically, starting from what was once Hackney Town, later part of

Church Street, and now forms that part of Mare Street north of the North London Line bridge. This area of Hackney has more illustrations and photographs than any other, and I have chosen to take the reader on a very long walk, in time and space, down the street, including some views that have not been published before and putting more familiar subjects into context. As it is not possible to incorporate contemporary photographs, I have tried to ensure that my locations are as precise as possible, so that the reader can make his or her own comparisons. The street- and place-names used are those that are contemporary with the image, but I have tried to give the modern name in brackets where appropriate. In the captions I have tried to give building dates and background information.

A selection of old photographs cannot be a history – in many cases the past is a lost place – but a guide is useful, even if the traveller does not choose to check every last entry against each place. I have also tried to avoid value judgements. It would be easy to make a case that Hackney was a more attractive place before the massive building development that took place from the mid-1870s onwards – but more attractive for whom? For example, the houses of the urban poor do not feature in picture postcard views. I have chosen to include a selection of slum clearance views from the 1930s as a reminder of what else we have lost besides elegant Georgian houses, tree-lined streets and gardens where the scent of the lilacs was especially strong.

There are two exceptions to the geographical theme. I considered a chapter on places of worship, but have chosen instead to scatter the religious among the secular, where each may benefit from the other. Nor is business wholly absent from the geographical excursions. Hackney's industrial past is in danger of becoming as forgotten as its rural past. Luckily, Hackney Archives Department has one of the largest collections of business records held by any of the London boroughs, and I have drawn on this to look at just a few employers, both major and minor. Similarly, the reader will find references to private schools scattered through the book, but the last chapter looks at two of Hackney's local authority secondary schools: one is still serving the community today; the other was closed under controversial circumstances.

Those who care to glance at the first and last entries will see that this book begins with hot air and ends with passion. Between the two at least something of human life in Hackney is there. If I have a passion myself, it is the relationship between image and place. This and previous works have depended heavily on the use of historical maps, including the facsimile series of the 25 inch to 1 mile series produced by Alan Godfrey. This book has also benefited from a computer database that is under construction at Hackney Archives Department. *Hackney on Disk* links text and images to the appropriate Ordnance Survey map. Users can search by keyword (for example, a subject like churches, or a specific street or building), and the maps can also be used to locate images. Drawing a box on a map allows the user to see a list of all of the images located in the area of the box. Division of the screen allows the image and the map to be displayed together, and a small red square indicates the location of each image. *Hackney on Disk* has been developed jointly with the National Trust's Sutton House, and the system, with as yet a limited amount of images, can be seen at Hackney Archives Department and Sutton House by prior arrangement. Subject to grant aid, it is hoped that the entire Hackney Archives Department collection will be put onto the database and that, in the future, the production of CD-ROMs with maps and selected images from the collection will be investigated.

David Mander
July 1996

A LONG WALK
DOWN MARE STREET

Mare Street was the principal thoroughfare in Hackney and it should be no surprise that it is the best illustrated of all of Hackney's roads. Before 1868 the name Mare Street applied only to the section south of today's Paragon Road. To the north was Church Street, named from the first St John at Hackney Church, the tower of which still stands behind the Old Town Hall. The shops in Church Street included printers and stationers, as well as early photographers like George James, operating from the mid-1860s. The products of pen, brush and camera have been included to provide a tour of a 150 years of Mare Street. This view shows the ford and two footbridges over the Hackney Brook, which crossed Church Street here on the line of the present Amhurst Road before bending north to run alongside Morning Lane. The small gateway in the centre marks the entrance to a lost mansion, the Black and White House. The seventeenth-century house to the left, refronted and rebuilt, lasted into the mid-Victorian period as a draper's shop.

We begin at the north end of Mare Street. The top view shows the junction with Dalston Lane and Ward's House, which was built by speculator John Ward shortly after 1711. Behind the house an extensive garden originally stretched back along Dalston Lane to the later Amhurst Road junction, bounded to the south by Hackney Brook. The bottom view, with the wall cut away, shows part of the garden and houses on the north side of Dalston Lane was built in the mid-1830s. Two watercolours by George Hawkins, late 1830s.

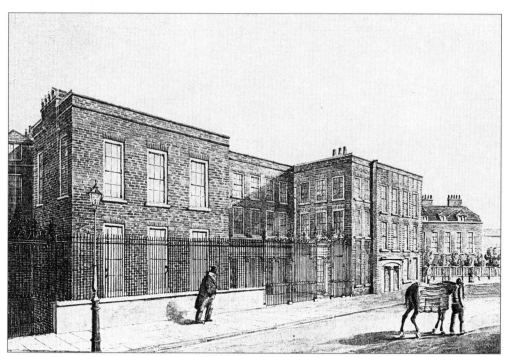

By the early nineteenth century Ward's House had been divided between four families, but it retained its unified appearance and fine railings. It was demolished *c*. 1847, and the lower view, a lithograph drawn by C.J. Greenwood in 1853, shows the shops on the right that replaced it. Crow's was probably a draper, while G. Bradley sold china and Mrs Harvey offered fancy goods.

The north end of Mare Street and the entrance to Hackney churchyard, late 1880s. Next to the churchyard was the police station in a building that appears to be a rebuild of the Bradley shop of the previous view, though the curved terrace of which it forms a part was built *c*. 1867. Samuel Morley's saddler's shop was next door from 1888 to the late 1890s. Hackney police station moved to its present accommodation in 1904.

A morning view, looking south, with the Kenmure Road junction on the right. The three balls belong to Robert Carter's pawnbroker's shop. Photograph by Alfred Braddock, 1886.

Looking north from 381 Mare Street, a George James photograph of about 1872, including the Manor House at no. 387 (with the prominent porch), then home to the Hackney Literary Institute but built in 1845 for J.R.D. Tyssen on the site of the Mermaid Assembly Rooms. The advert for Ibbetson's tea was a recent addition to the wall of Wilkinson's grocery – literally a sign of things to come.

The former Manor House has become Lilley and Skinner's shoe shop and a gas mantle shop, and advertising abounds in this photograph by Alfred Braddock of 1904. The horse trams were to give way to electric successors in 1909.

Thomas Rowlandson had his own view of polite Hackney in 1812. 'The Graces, the Graces, remember the Graces' was his caption to this 1812 view of Hackney Assembly Rooms. Incorporating the site and grounds of Hackney's original Rectory, the new Mermaid and its pleasure gardens included the Assembly Rooms, founded before 1744 to address what Dudley Ryder, the local diarist of 1716, had described as the lack of 'sociableness or familiarity kept up between families'. They were rebuilt by Antony Brunn, lessee of the Mermaid from 1766, who was advertising seasonal balls there in his new rooms in the late 1770s. Although the new Mermaid itself made way for Tyssen's new house in 1845, the Assembly Rooms were approached by a long covered passageway from just north of the Manor House. The grounds to the south, site of early nineteenth-century balloon ascents, had been built over by 1877, but the Assembly Rooms lasted until 1891 when Kenmure Avenue was created. A successor building, the Manor Theatre, on the corner of Brett and Kenmure Roads was to become a cinema by 1913 and the Hackney Radical Club in the 1920s.

The Templars' House had long fallen into multi-occupancy when this watercolour of about 1800 was made. The projecting centre bay with the Ionic columns, broken pediments and two side pediments had originally been capped by domes similar to those on Hatfield House, suggesting that it was either built in the later part of the sixteenth century or altered from an earlier building. The Templars' name came from the estate of that order in Hackney, which later became Kingshold Manor. One of the earliest of Hackney's private schools was established in 1643 by Mary Perwich, occupying a thirty-six hearth house, which may have been at the north end of Church Street, and so could have been the Templars' House. Mary's daughter Susanna was a noted violinist and attracted a distinguished audience from London. The house became a tavern, the Blue Posts, *c.* 1750 and was used by the Vestry as a meeting place to conduct parish business. The southern part of Lower Clapton Road was once Bob's Hall Lane from the alternative name for the house. After 1777 the landlord, a Mr Wright, built an assembly room at the rear, which survived the demolition of the old house (said by Benjamin Clarke the antiquarian to have occurred between 1825 and 1827, though a building very like the Templar's House still appears on the 1831 map of Hackney).

The Black and White House, stood just to the south of the Old Church. This watercolour of *c.* 1780 shows the white or garden side and the one opposite the Brown Room (presumably at the front of the house) not long before demolition in 1796. The front or black side of the house was half timbered. Said to date from 1578, the house was bought by the Lord Mayor of London, Sir Thomas Vyner, and altered so that in 1684 it was the second largest house in Church Street after the Perwich School. Stained glass just visible in the picture opposite included the coat of arms of Frederick V and his consort, Elizabeth, daughter of James I, who may have stayed here after their brief period as rulers of Bohemia in 1618. The house was purchased by the Ryder family in 1706. For more than 100 years from about 1688 it was another of Hackney's many private schools. The site became Bohemia Place – the present roadway to the bus garage.

Church Street, looking north from near the present Graham Road junction, from a drawing by Robert Schnebbelie published in 1805. The bridge over Hackney Brook was constructed by a group of local gentlemen and funded by subscription – the various bodies governing Hackney declined to aid the project financially. The obelisk may have commemorated this, or have been a mile post, but it appears to have been short-lived. The passageway alongside the bridge led to a mid-seventeenth-century house owned by William Spurstowe and today is the site of the Amhurst Road junction.

South front of William Spurstowe's house, early 1800s. Spurstowe was vicar of Hackney from 1643 to 1662, when he became one of the ejected ministers who refused to accept the terms of the Act of Uniformity of 1662. He acquired an estate on the west side of Church Street which included this house just east of the confluence of Hackney and Pigwell brooks. It was the third largest of the Church Street houses in 1664. Spurstowe also founded almshouses on a site behind the present-day Hackney Empire. The estate was sold by his descendants in 1719. The owner of one part from 1761 was army surgeon Sir John Silvester, who employed the young German gardener Conrad Loddiges to remodel the grounds, replacing the formal ornamental canals with five cascades, a Chinese bridge, a grotto and a Gothic hermitage. Silvester also built five houses in what was to become Silvester Row (now Sylvester Row). The house and grounds were sold to Richard Dann, who already owned the other part of the estate, and his family enlarged the house *c.* 1800. A later owner was retired silversmith William Nelme who was poisoned by his grandson in 1847. By then called Park House, the building was used as an Islington pauper children's home from 1849 to 1862, when it was demolished for the construction of Amhurst Road. The terrace that is now 1–19 Amhurst Road was built on the site, though the first attempt, by a Mr Amos, collapsed and had to be rebuilt.

The bridge area of Church Street, dating from a little later than the view on p. 17, possibly drawn in the 1820s. The buildings on the left beyond the bridge have lost their weatherboarding and, judging by the lines on the road, there was a fair degree of mud about. Street lights have also appeared. Church Street was part of the road network controlled by the Hackney Turnpike Trust from 1738 to 1827. The trust provided oil-lamps from 1755, their lighting powers devolved onto the parish after 1763. In March 1767 Hackney's Lighting and Watching Trustees formed a committee to inform the Turnpike Trustees of 'the hardship to the inhabitants to light the turnpike through the Town of Hackney at the expense of the parish', but presumably the parish had to continue to meet the costs and pay the lamplighters. Gas lighting came in from the 1820s, but Hackney's last oil lamps were not converted to gas until 1857.

This 1835 view was drawn by George Hawkins, from a point a little south of the previous view. Hackney had a stagecoach link with Bishopsgate from 1740 and one has just set down by the gates to Park House. Omnibus services started *c.* 1838. The shop marked Late Holmes is Slatterie and Green's draper's shop, later Green and Branscombe, and is the building that appears in the left of the picture on page 9. Alterations involved the removal of the side gable, and the substitution of a new front and sash windows. Benjamin Clarke visited the house in 1893 and was struck by the substantial oak staircase, with heavily carved banister and rail, which led up into a dormered roof supported 'by a perfect labyrinth of oaken beams and stays'. Rooms on the first floor were intermingled with narrow passages. Between this house and the ornamental railings was a narrow passage that later became Brook Place. Behind the railings was a double-fronted late seventeenth-century house that was home in the 1820s to William Hare, who had once been Hackney's only surgeon. In common with many in his profession, Hare had begun as an apothecary, which did not require qualifications. In 1831 he had seven inmates staying with him, presumably residential patients?

The 1850s began a substantial period of change for Mare Street, some of which can be seen in this C.J. Greenwood lithograph of 1853. The East and West India Docks and Birmingham Junction Railway was authorized in 1846 to build a line from Camden Town to Blackwall. Construction was completed in 1850 and in 1853 the company was renamed the North London Railway. Construction of the line on a raised viaduct through the centre of Hackney did considerable damage. A house with features that suggest a sixteenth-century building date were demolished on the west side of the road, three houses on the east were pulled down and the bridge broke up the line of Church Street. The engine is hauling four-wheeled stock; passengers were not transported on bogie stock until after the takeover by the London and North Western Railway in 1909. Hackney's first station was on the east side of the road, replaced by a new one to the west in 1870. The King's Head public house appears to have been weatherboarded in this view; it was a timber-framed building, possibly dating from the sixteenth century, and was to last (weatherboarding removed) until 1878. Alongside are Bonter's the fishmonger's, Tuck's the pastrycook and King's the cheesemonger's. The three women are outside Jay's the upholsterer's. On the left, Brook Place and the shops have replaced Mr Hare's old house.

A horse and cart wait patiently by W.S. Richards the corn dealer's under the tree at the corner of Hackney Churchyard. Further along are the Old Town Hall of 1802 and Dennis Brothers' grocer's shop. There are no tram tracks, so this George James photograph probably dates from around 1870. The Old Town Hall had ceased to be the seat of Hackney's local government in 1866 and now housed the Hackney Bank for Savings, founded in 1818, which was to last until 1894.

The Mare Street frontage to Matthew Rose's draper's shop around 1868. Rose had taken over an established drapers business at London House around 1852 and expanded into the neighbouring shops. In 1868 the premises were extended backwards to provide new shops on Amhurst Road, claimed to be more convenient for the carriage trade, which would have found the problem of parking in this narrow part of Mare Street difficult, even then!

The Mare Street frontage to Matthew Rose's draper's shop, *c*. 1868. Rose had taken over an established draper's business at London House *c*. 1852 and expanded into the neighbouring shops. In 1868 the premises were extended backwards to provide new shops on Amhurst Road, which was claimed to be more convenient for the carriage trade, which would have had a problem parking in this narrow part of Mare Street even then.

A sale in full swing at Matthew Rose's shop, in the summer of 1908. Rose used the enforced road widening of 1877 to enlarge the Mare Street frontage sideways and upwards. The new building took in the former site of the Eight Bells and shops to the north, and the extra floors allowed the business to expand into furniture, carpets, china and glass, ironmongery and house removals, becoming in effect Hackney's principal department store. The Rose family had given up living above the shop some time before, and drapery profits paid for a fine house in the Loughton area. Horse traffic and trams still form the bulk of the sparse traffic. The electric streetlight was a product of Hackney's electricity programme. The council had its own power station, opened in 1901. Matthew Rose's business closed in 1936 and the premises were rebuilt by Marks and Spencer shortly afterwards. Photograph by Alfred Braddock.

Hackney Churchyard and the rear of the Old Town Hall, were painted around 1830 by George Hawkins. A passageway at this end of the churchyard was ordered to be made by Hackney's Vestry in 1657, at the expense of John Wetherhead's hog sty. The accompanying description suggests that there were no houses between the old church and the Black and White House, suggesting the cottage and two houses with Georgian fronts that faced the churchyard date from the second half of the seventeenth century. Still there in the late 1860s, they were rebuilt in 1882. The shops on Church Street are the pair to the north of the draper's that was to become Matthew Rose's first shop. Originally the Old Town Hall had only one storey and a loft. In 1825 it was altered to provide a second floor (the Trustees of the Poor who were responsible also insisted on plenty of hat pegs and 'the necessary stoves'). The new building held the parish watch (replaced by the Metropolitan Police after 1829), a fire engine and the Superintendent Registrar of Births, Marriages and Deaths. The functionary lurking in the back doorway may have been the attendant, passing the time of day with two local women.

A cab waits for custom in the cab stand at the Church Street end of Amhurst Road, in this photograph by George James of *c.* 1866. The site alongside the corner house, once gardens of the Church Street houses, stretching down to the Hackney Brook, was soon to become the extension to Matthew Rose's store, which opened in 1868.

By the early 1870s the covered passageway and studio window of the end house on the Amhurst Road corner had given way to an extension to F.G. Winny's haberdasher's shop. Over the road, Albion House formed the emporium of W. Barker, the tailors. Photograph by George James, *c.* 1872.

A Hackney lounger poses against Mr Winny's door for George James' camera in this view of Nos 341–3, Mare Street in 1872. Next to Winny's are W. Newman, house decorator, and Robert Barker, stationer and bookseller, with a coal merchant squeezed in at no. 345 alongside the Eight Bells public house. This little row of timber-framed buildings received a new brick front, possibly in the 1820s, and was demolished for the road widening of 1875–77.

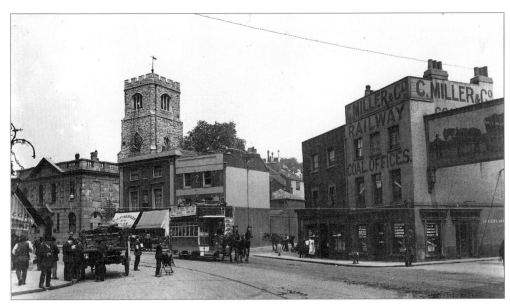

A horse tram waits by Bohemia Place and another horse is led from the depot, in this Alfred Braddock view of *c.* 1900. The Old Town Hall has recently become a branch of the Midland Bank, which had the whole building clad in stone (only the front was stone-clad previously). Dennis's shop has long since changed hands, but the front retains the beehive relief between the first floor windows. The yard alongside the offices of Miller's Coal led to railway sidings, which were still in place in the early 1960s.

Nos 342–346 Mare Street, *c.* 1888. J.B. Brodribb was a chemist, with a doctor's surgery above, and William Dinmore's coffee rooms were next door. All of these houses were destroyed in the Blitz on the night of 19/20 March 1941. Photograph by Alfred Braddock.

The shops of William Smith the tailor and George Cox, baker, stood on the west side of Church Street at the point where the North London railway viaduct was to cross. This elevation and plan were made not long before they were demolished in 1849. The design of the bay would suggest that it and the rest of the building dated from the sixteenth or early seventeenth century; whoever commissioned the drawing recognised that something of interest was to be lost and should be recorded, ensuring that an image, if not the buildings themselves, survived.

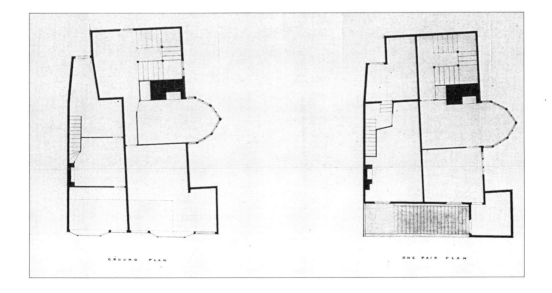

A last look up Church Street one late summer afternoon, through the lens of George James around 1869. The small cart probably belongs to a street trader.

George James has turned south to include the Eight Bells, the railway bridge, and the shops beyond, also about 1869. Road widening south of the bridge in 1904 replaced these shops with the present four-storey row.

The waters of the Hackney Brook, which had been channelled into watercress beds, just to the south of the railway, looking from Morning Lane, 1853. The supports and line of contractor's wagons alongside the North London Railway viaduct suggest that widening was in progress to put in an extra loop. In the mid-1840s the beds were farmed by Thomas Hayward, whose cottage may be the building visible alongside the trees. Beyond is the end of the Georgian Church Field House, the garden of which fronted on to the churchyard. The site of the house and garden were used to build the North Metropolitan Tramways depot in 1872. Increasing problems with sewage in the Hackney Brook were demonstrated when one of Hayward's daughters fell into a pond and was temporarily trapped by the tenacious and foul-smelling mud under the water's surface. Eventually the water supply from the brook was replaced by well water. The watercress beds were taken over to build Chalgrove Road in 1875, which was bombed on the night of 19/20 March 1941. Today the site is a car park. Watercolour by T.C. Dibdin.

Two photographs by George James from just south of the Kings Head, 1869, with Green and Branscombe's shop in the centre in each. It has been rebuilt and refronted since 1853. In 1872 the shops in the lower view included a corndealer, a 'fancy depot', a milliner's and W.G. Fish, the long-established pawnbroker's, later to move across the road.

From almost the same position as the view on the left, Alfred Braddock took this view in 1887. Graham Road was completed in 1875 and the gabled buildings, which were built after that date, have given the street a much more urban feel. The Cock was not rebuilt until 1930.

Alfred Braddock must have got up early to take this view in 1884, which includes the rebuilt King's Head (right). Eley and Wilmer the draper's was to house Henry Mason's cinematographic exhibition in 1909, one of the earliest cinemas in Hackney. No. 333, part of the double-gabled building on the left, was the Hackney Picture Palace by 1911, though both this and no. 329, the former Green and Branscombe's shop before the bridge were given over to the Hackney Furnishing Company, no. 329 was later demolished to widen Graham Road.

Looking north from the Britannia public house, another George James view of *c.* 1872. This view includes the small shops that were demolished for the construction of the Hackney Empire, which opened in 1901.

Looking north from the Cock, 1906. The full range of turn-of-the-century traffic is represented, from a brougham to a motor car. It appears that the old Green and Branscombe shop is in the course of alteration. Photograph by Alfred Braddock.

The Hackney Empire and Empire Mansions, were all decorated on 28 May 1908 in honour of the visit of the Prince and Princess of Wales to open the new Hackney Central Library. An attempt to establish a free library in 1878 had been defeated in a rowdy public meeting, and it was not until 1903 that Hackney Metropolitan Borough adopted the Public Libraries Act. The new library was designed by Henry Crouch and was built on land left over after the widening of Mare Street, with financial assistance from Andrew Carnegie.

Inside the new Hackney Central Library, 28 May 1908. Invited guests are waiting expectantly. A select few, including former mayors, their consorts, alderman and local MPs, were formally presented to the Prince and Princess of Wales in the News Room on the ground floor. Other guests appear to have been seated in upper rooms of the library.

Views up and down the Top Hall of Hackney Central Library on the same day. This hall could be used for lectures, and it later became the reference library. A selection of local children were gathered in the Children's Library to sing 'God Bless the Prince of Wales'. There was also music from the Francis Bijou Orchestra. Meanwhile, in the top hall, everyone is waiting. Not long now. . .

Cab and cart wait for Vestry and any other custom outside Hackney's second town hall at election time, May 1868. Built in 1866 in the centre of Hackney Grove in a French-Italian style and designed by Hammack and Lambert, this building soon proved to be too small for the expanding Vestry and its officers. In the background is the Britannia public house, first established around 1825. Photograph by George James.

A winter scene outside the town hall, in 1900–1901, with a horse tram trotting northwards. The town hall was extended to the designs of Gordon, Lowther and Gunton, with two new wings completed in 1898. It was demolished in 1937 as the present town hall rose behind it. The Hackney Empire in the background had just been completed.

One of Hackney's lost houses is the White House, which may once have been the property of Sir Thomas Marsh (d. 1677). This George James view of about 1868 shows an old gabled house on that site in the course of demolition, with builders and local people posing for the camera.. Benjamin Clarke thought that it stood at the north-east corner of Baxters Court, a lost alley on the east side of Mare Street, opposite the Britannia public house.

Jerusalem Square lay to the south of Baxter's Court, linked to Paragon Road by a long alley called Jerusalem Passage, running roughly on the line of the present Valette Street. This view of about 1895 shows the north side of a small terrace dated 1708 (from the plaque in the centre). The edge of Jerusalem Passage is on the left. Houses in the passage were also old – a former inhabitant writing in 1934 recalled costers trundling their barrows along the narrow pathway. A small local beerhouse was the meeting place for most of the shoemakers in Hackney to play skittles and engage in fierce domino contests, with the losers meeting the cost of a sheep's head supper. The same author recalled the atmosphere: 'the old place was not too well lighted. Two or three dim gas lamps, fixed into iron brackets attached to the walls of the houses were the only illuminants . . . To walk through Jerusalem Passage on a winter's night when the old buildings were covered with a mantle of snow was to experience the fascinating impression and atmosphere which only those old world corners can convey – that you were strolling through a bit of old London.' Both the square and the passage, with its houses with windows almost at floor level, were cleared for the Valette Street redevelopment not long after this photograph was taken.

Looking north from just south of the Richmond Road junction in 1870. George James had no problems with traffic when he stood in the road to take this photograph. Benjamin Clarke was to complain of the vigour with which Hackney Board of Works removed trees from Mare Street. Those on the left are in the back gardens of the former King's Row, the houses on the south side of Hackney Grove.

The Ivy House and its neighbouring pair of villas stood just north of the Richmond Road junction, and are partially visible in the James photograph above. This view of about 1910 was taken from just across the road. The Ivy House was leased to Benjamin Smith, who built nos 273–275 Mare Street next door in 1838. Used by the Salvation Army from 1894, the Ivy House was demolished in 1926 and the neighbouring villas in 1972 suffered the same fate after being used as a clothing factory.

Looking north from the Paragon Road junction, late 1860s. J.Corby, the vet's, house is in front of Child's Forge on the corner. J.W.Whelan's tiny gas fitter's shop next door was at 242 Mare Street and a few doors down another J. Whelan kept an ironmonger's. These shops disappeared *c.* 1907 to allow the construction of Hackney's first public library (1908), the Methodist Central Hall (1924) and the adjoining Salvation Army citadel (1910). Photograph by George James.

Looking north towards Richmond Road junction. A dray has stopped by the Horse and Groom public house in this decidedly busy scene of about 1905, looking north towards the Richmond Road junction. The pub has recently become 'Hobson's Choice'!

A rather gloomy view of the houses on the southern corner of the Richmond Road junction, *c*. 1900. In the 1890s nos 267–269 were private houses, no. 269 being the residence of surgeon Edward Dennis Hacon, almost certainly the son of South Hackney resident Hylton Dennis Hacon, who was responsible for a vanished terrace on the south side of Well Street and similar houses in King Edward's and Tudor Roads. By 1905, shops had been built on the front gardens, which survive today, although the houses appear to have been bomb damaged and had gone by 1949. Just visible on Richmond Road is the Methodist Chapel of 1846. This closed in 1925 when the new Central Hall opened. It was used as a synagogue until 1938. Intended to be converted for factory use, the building was also bombed and the site was used for a new factory in 1954.

Barber's Barn stood just to the south of the present Darnley Road junction. There was a building on this site in 1539, when land in this area of Mare Street formed part of the reputed manor of Shoreditch Place and was held by the hospital of the Savoy from the Hospitallers. The Savoy Hospital was dissolved in 1539 and its lands passed to St Thomas Hospital. The house in this view was said to date from c. 1590. It was a timber-framed house with plaster details on the sides. In the Commonwealth period it was leased to the regicide Col. John Okey, who had been a drayman and a stoker in an Islington brewhouse and who had a rather good war. Okey fled abroad on the restoration of Charles II, but was captured in Holland and brought back to England to be executed in 1662. His widow was allowed to keep the house. By the date of this drawing of c. 1790, Barbers Barn was one of Hackney's many private schools and was kept by a Mr Worsley. Much of the adjoining land was leased to nurseryman Conrad Loddiges. In 1792, Loddiges acquired the old house and later built a terrace to help towards the costs of developing what was to become a celebrated nursery until its closure in 1852.

Mrs Wingrove's ironmonger's shop, 229 Mare Street, *c.* 1872. This shop stood just to the south of London Lane. This view includes the entrance to the south to the courtyard of the Nag's Head public house. The house was refronted in the nineteenth century but may have dated from the late seventeenth century. In 1775 Conrad Loddiges set up his first small nursery and seed shop on the opposite corner, and issued his first catalogue two years later. Photograph by George James.

The south side of London Lane, with the side wall of 229 Mare Street, *c* 1872. The Nag's Head had an additional frontage on London Lane until 1875, when all of these houses were demolished and the Nag's Head was rebuilt. Photograph by George James.

William Sharman's chemist and dentist business, 186 Mare Street. Sharman's business was established in the early 1890s and he moved in 1898 to 186 Mare Street on the northern corner of St Thomas Square. The house was badly damaged by bombing on 9 September 1940 and the site now forms the grounds of Pitcairn House.

On the south side of St Thomas Square was the Independent Chapel of 1772 with its own burial ground. The house beyond was the original minister's house and was altered c. 1875, losing its projecting frontage at the same time that the Catholic Apostolic Church was constructed in the minister's garden alongside (marked by the trees). The St Thomas Square Chapel became a cinema in 1914 and was later rebuilt. In 1996 a new residential block for Cordwainers College was under construction. The Catholic Apostolic Church was sold to a Greek Orthodox congregation in 1966.

Elm House, later 219 Mare Street, when it was on the verge of demolition, *c*. 1900. The house had been in industrial use for around thirty years at this time. In 1872 it was a carmine makers and it was probably this business that added the extension used as a cycle works. The substantial houses along Mare Street were gradually giving way to shops and industrial premises in the later nineteenth century.

No. 193 Mare Street, was a villa just to the south of the Elizabeth Fry Refuge which is now the Lansdowne Club and Mare Street's only surviving domestic building from the first half of the eighteenth century. The deceptively simple plastered front of no. 193 hid a timber-framed building, dated by Benjamin Clarke to the sixteenth century. A tiny shop that stood in the garden had gone by this time. Clarke recalled that the house and its spacious front garden with flowering trees was several steps below street level. Inside, the rooms were large but with low ceilings, and the long back garden had a fine mulberry tree in it. No. 193 made way for the construction of Fortescue Avenue in 1880. Photograph by George James, *c*. 1870.

In 1900 no. 172 Mare Street was a coffee house, but in 1815 these premises were Hackney's first chemist, which was taken on four years later by Benjamin Clarke Snr, the antiquarian's father. Alongside is Pemberton Place Cottages, the first of whose houses date back to 1834 when the court was built on the site of a large timber yard. Pemberton Place remains, but the chemist had gone by 1905.

In 1900 the east side of Mare Street south of the Well Street junction consisted of these rows of late seventeenth- and early eighteenth-century houses, with extended shopfronts. There were shops here in the 1840s. Thomas Coish Staddon's draper's shop had recently expanded into nos 138–140. The diarist and traveller Celia Fiennes (1662–1741) was living in one of these houses at her death, having come to Hackney to be near her nieces, though Hackney's strong nonconformist community would have suited her own religious views. From her will it appears that she had a maid, a cook and up to five other servants. Her furniture included Japan and tortoiseshell cabinets, couches and easy chairs, one on wheels.

This George James photograph of about 1870 shows the west side of Mare Street at the junction with Helmsley Place, *c.* 1870. In the foreground is 155 Mare Street, which was used by surgeons in 1872 and was demolished to build the present bank on the site in 1903. To the north and standing back from the road is Pembroke House, which was used as an asylum by the East India Company from 1818 to 1870. It was bought by the Great Eastern Railway and shops were built on the site by prolific local builder William Osment in 1873.

Looking south towards the Triangle, *c.* 1900. Osment's shops are on the right and beyond the bank are the trees in front of Mare Street Baptist Church. The tall building in the distance is Morley Hall of 1879.

The first Mare Street Baptist Church, built in 1811, burned down in 1854. The new church, in an imposing Classical style, was designed by W.G. & E. Habershon to seat 1,200 and this print by W.G. Habershon of about 1855 was intended to show the finished product. It opened on the same site as its predecessor, just south of Helmsley Place, and was demolished after bomb and rocket damage in 1940 and 1945. The houses to the left lay in front of the Flying Horse Inn.

Exmouth Place originally ran from 149 Mare Street through to London Fields. This view of *c.* 1886 may be the west end, showing the yard shared by a van proprietor and Charles Jones's bill poster business at No. 18 (the plastered bills being examples of his trade). If this is so, the row behind the two small shops is Helmsley Terrace, later London Fields East Side. Some of the shops were in use by boot and shoe makers by 1890. However, the map evidence is inconclusive and this terrace is wrong for this site. Other suggestions are welcome.

The Flying Horse Inn straddling Exmouth Place, and the range of which this inn was a part was in poor condition when this photograph of about 1909 was taken. The original inn lay on the left of the picture, and a lane (known as Flying Horse Yard in 1831) ran towards a small row of houses looking on to London Fields called Exmouth Place. The Flying Horse was in existence in 1708, when the Vestry met to audit the local government expenses of the year, and was thought by Benjamin Clarke to have been an Elizabethan posting house. The south side of the range was demolished shortly after this photograph was taken. The Flying Horse ceased to be a pub before 1914, though the building still survived in 1930.

(*Opposite, top*) The Mare Street branch of the London and Provincial Bank, corner of King Edward's Road, viewed from the other side of the Triangle in 1905. The gates on the left of the bank led to St Joseph's Roman Catholic Church. The bank was one of a number of large commercial buildings built on Mare Street in the late 1890s. This part of the street was badly bombed and the church and the bank were destroyed. The branch was rebuilt after the war by Barclays Bank, though it has since closed.

(*Opposite, bottom*) The Triangle marked the junction with West Street and the southern section of Mare Street, known as Cambridge Heath until 1868. In the centre was a small green. This late eighteenth-century drawing shows Albion House, which from 1789, was one of Hackney's many private schools. It stood on the south side of the Triangle. A gutter head on the house was dated 1656, though the property may have dated from even earlier. From 1801 to 1806 the school was kept by Mrs Perry. Leased to builder William Lucas in 1824, the house was then demolished and nos 111–113 Mare Street built on the site.

South side of the Triangle, *c.* 1900. The pair of houses on the left are nos 115–117 Mare Street, which were built in 1856. Next to them is the first house in West Street, owned for many years by the Willmot family, who were builders. The Willmotts appear to have owned other houses in this part of West Street. The antiquarian Benjamin Clarke claimed that the Collis Willmott residence in 1893 (by which he may have meant this house) dated from 1600. If this was the case, the house seems to have been refronted in the early eighteenth century. West Street became Westgate Street in 1911. All of the buildings on the south side of Westgate Street east of the railway bridge were destroyed by a V-1 on 29 July 1944. Netil House and Keltan House now stand on the site.

The east side of Mare Street opposite the Triangle, a George James view of *c.* 1870. A hansom cab and a corn dealer's wagon are waiting by the cab stand. The small row of shops dates from the 1830s onwards. The spire and garden belong to St Joseph's Roman Catholic Church, which was built to the design of W.W. Wardell in 1847–8. There was a school at the rear. The present church dates from 1956, as the original was destroyed in the Second World War.

Looking north from the Regent's Canal Bridge, this postcard of around 1905 includes (left) Victoria Mansions (of 1887) and the Rose and Crown, which had its own small pleasure garden in the 1830s. The pub was rebuilt after a fire before 1856 and altered in 1891.

In the 1830s the eastern end of the present Andrews Road formed the end of Sheep Lane and its few houses included a large villa on the north side. The completion of the Regents Canal just to the south in 1820 led to the development of gas works on the Bethnal Green side and made the area less attractive, and the villa was acquired by the British Penitent Female Refuge, a body founded in 1829 to reclaim and resettle prostitutes. The top view dates from the 1860s, before the construction of the Great Eastern Railway line from Liverpool Street in 1872. By 1881 the house had become one of the homes of the King Edward Certified Industrial School, and the gardens at the rear were built over. The lower view of about 1905 has been carefully cropped to leave out the railway bridge, which ran immediately to the right. The property survives today as Cintique's furniture factory and, although altered, retains its pediment.

HOMERTON INTERLUDE

Homerton was once divided into Upper and Lower Homerton. 'Upper' was the present Urswick Road and 'Lower' was the High Street ('Homerton' was not added until 1935), which gradually descended to Marsh Hill, running north of the line of the Hackney Brook. In the seventeenth century, Homerton was the most populous of the Hackney settlements and attracted a number of wealthy courtiers in the sixteenth century, including Ralph Sadleir (1507–87), diplomat and builder of Sutton House, Thomas Sutton (d. 1611), the founder of the Charterhouse and reputedly the richest commoner of his day, and Lord Zouche (d. 1625), who employed Matthias L'Obel (from whom the Lobelia takes its name) to care for his physic garden. Our Homerton interlude begins at the west end of Sutton Place. This watercolour by George Hawkins, of about 1830, shows the Hackney Proprietary Grammar School, founded in that year. It would not admit children of local shopkeepers, and this led to the foundation of a rival school in Clarence Road. The two schools merged in 1848, after which this building became Sutton Lodge. Incorporated into the Metal Box factory, the former school was demolished c. 1960.

Churchwell Path (named after the well) links Morning Lane with Clapton, running along the east side of the churchyard. This sketch of *c*. 1825 is taken just north of the well and includes the backs of the houses on the south side of Sutton Place. These had been built around 1809 under a lease granted to William Collins, replacing the Tan House, which may have been Thomas Sutton's Hackney residence.

Sutton House, 1880s. This house was built *c*. 1535 for Sir Ralph Sadleir and was originally called the Bryk Place. Like many Hackney houses it has served as a private school. In 1741–3 it received its present Georgian front, and *c*. 1751 it was divided into two houses. The trees almost obscure the frontage, but just show the original sash windows. The present ones represent what late nineteenth-century craftsmen felt Georgian windows should look like.

Sutton House, 1928. In 1890 both parts of Sutton House were bought by the Rector of Hackney, Arthur Lawley, and altered internally to become St John's Church Institute, which was intended to provide a place of study and leisure for Hackney's working men. Bedrooms were provided for young men, including visiting missionary clergy, to lodge. The top view shows one of the bedrooms on the second floor (now used as the Archive Room for the *Hackney on Disk* project). The bottom view shows a sitting room on the ground floor (now the Georgian Parlour). When the institute moved out in 1936 the house was put up for sale. After an appeal, in which the Labour MP for Poplar, George Lansbury, took an active part, could not raise sufficient funds to buy it, Sutton House was acquired by the National Trust in 1938.

Earlscroft and Earlsmead were paired eighteenth-century houses on the west side of Upper Homerton, just south of the junction with the present St John's Church Road. In the 1870s the plot on the opposite side of the road may have been a paddock, with a raised mound crowned with trees. This Alfred Braddock view was taken long before both houses were demolished in 1882 for the development that included the now vanished Halidon Road. Just visible in the distance is Ram's Episcopal Infant School, which was built in 1877.

Looking from the west end of Homerton Row, 1884. On the south (right) side is a Baptist Chapel of 1822 (closed between 1959 and 1964). Beyond is the new Homerton Row Board School, which was built in 1883 and demolished before 1982, when the new Homerton House School was built. The tall chimneys (left) mark the houses that formed the original Homerton Row, which dated from the early eighteenth century and were demolished in 1887. Photograph by Alfred Braddock.

The Gravel Pit Chapel Hall and Mission Rooms stood at the north-east end of Homerton Grove, and were photographed by Alfred Braddock *c.* 1888. Built in 1862, the mission was short lived, for the site was taken for the ambulance station of the Eastern Hospital in 1884/5. Claimed as the first built for that purpose in England, the ambulance station is itself threatened with demolition in 1996.

Homerton High Street, looking east, *c.* 1870. This was something of a backwater before the 1880s. This George James view shows the junction with Plough (now Furrow) Lane and the fine timber-framed range that included the Plough public house at its western end which originally stretched from Plough Lane to the now vanished Bannister Street. On the right the junction with Bridge Street (now Ponsford Street) is just visible.

Homerton High Street, looking west, *c*. 1830. This shows the same range as before from the opposite direction. In 1831 the shops here included a butcher's, a draper's and, in the foreground, a greengrocer's. The tree in front of the shop was to survive until the buildings were demolished. Watercolour by George Hawkins.

The eastern end of the High Street range to the junction with John (later Bannister) Street, a watercolour of 1840. Benjamin Clarke suggested that the line of the gables should be recreated in a new building as an echo of the splendid range. Demolition began at this end and all but the Plough had gone by 1887.

Homerton High Street, *c*. 1892. The Plough had also been rebuilt by this time. Further rebuilding followed in 1898. The house on the other side of Plough Lane was divided between an oil shop (no. 19) and, on the corner, a marine store (no. 21). Beyond, the group of black-clad women has just passed Ram's Episcopal Chapel of 1723. No. 19 and probably no. 21 were rebuilt in 1904.

High Street and Ponsford Street, looking east. Much of the south side of the High Street near the Ponsford Street junction was open land in 1950, the result of a combination of bombing and the prewar slum clearance programme. Here the sharp bend in the road and the original width of Ponsford Street are visible, both of which were altered in a major road scheme in 1960. The foreground now forms part of Marian Court.

No. 79 Homerton High Street, c. 1900. This was a grocery and one of a pair of shops on the corner of College Street. The premises were rebuilt in 1901. Two locally produced products are prominently displayed: Clarnicos' cocoa was produced by Clarke, Nickolls and Coombs in Wallis Road, and Batey's gingerbeer was made just south of the Kingsland Road canal bridge.

Before and after views of the south side of High Street from the Ponsford Street junction. The top photograph was taken in 1886, when roof repairs were under way at C.R. Heward's ironmongery. In the bottom view of 1905, new shops have replaced a removal man's yard and adjoining businesses. Joseph Olley the butcher and other locals obligingly paused and posed. Photographs by Alfred Braddock.

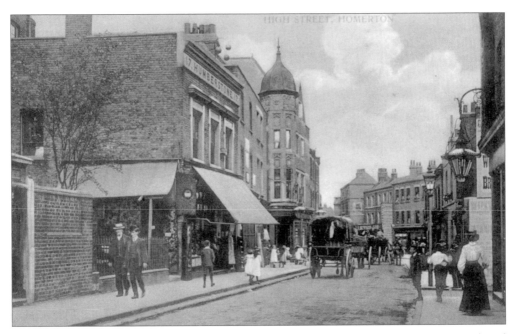

Looking west from near the junction with Marian Street (right), *c.* 1900. On the left, Edward Humberstone's pawnbroking business, established before 1867, had been let to Bliss and Norton, though the parapet sign remained. The turret belongs to the rebuilt Plough public house.

St Barnabas's vicarage and church were well screened from the road by trees in 1870. The church was completed in 1847, having been designed by Arthur Ashpitel, who was also responsible for the vicarage. The church was bomb damaged in 1944 and then altered before rededication in 1958. In 1981 St Barnabas's parish was combined with a former daughter church, St Paul's, Glyn Road (1889), and the combined congregations ensured the survival of St Barnabas's Church as a place of worship. Photograph by George James.

The High Street, looking west from near the Sedgwick Street junction. The tall houses on the left, nos 142–144, date from the early nineteenth century and survive today. A postcard by Charles Martin, c. 1905

Looking west, from the junction with Crozier Terrace, c. 1905. The shops adjoining St Barnabas's Church are on the site of Homerton Library, which was opened in 1974. Postcard by Charles Martin.

High Street and Marian Street junction. Slum clearance was planned in the Homerton area in the mid-1930s. This official photograph of houses on either side of the High Street junction with Marian Street shows what was marked for destruction. The entire south side of Homerton High Street was renumbered in 1910, hence the apparent duplication in numbering with the houses shown on page 65. Marian Court now occupies the site of nos 56–66.

Homerton Station, looking south, 1905. The construction of the North London Railway in 1850 cut through the open land to the east of Ponsford (Link) Street and south of the High Street. This was one factor in the social decline of Homerton. Homerton Station opened in 1868, with the single-storey station building on Church (later Barnabas) Road. The station is on the right with the signal box above the bridge.

Bannister Street began life as Chapel Street, changing its name to John Street by the mid-1840s and the houses north of the bend were probably built around 1830. When this view was taken in the early 1930s, looking north towards Homerton Grove, the area was designated for slum clearance. The building on the left served as Homerton Ragged School from 1871–5, when it was taken over as a Board School. Bannister House, which now covers the site, was completed in 1935.

Nisbet Street on the south side of Homerton High Street, looking south towards the North London Railway line, early 1930s. Built in 1871, the area was cleared c. 1935 and Nisbet House was opened in 1938.

In common with many other parishes, Hackney Parish provided a workhouse for paupers. On the south side of Homerton High Street a timber-framed house dating from the sixteenth century was leased in 1741 from the Milborne family and bought in 1769. The original drawing of 1841 copied here had a flap, which has been dropped to show the house front (top view). The buildings to the right were gradually added by the parish, as the pauper population increased, and eventually extended, all round the back of the old house (bottom view from middle of yard.) The workhouse was not always directly run by the parish. In the 1760s there were periods when it was leased to a contractor, though eventually the parish discovered that it could do the job more effectively itself. In 1831, 102 men, 153 women, 80 boys and 60 girls lived here. After the newly formed Hackney Board of Guardians took over, the old buildings were demolished (c. 1841) and replaced by a new workhouse, which became Hackney Hospital in 1930. Watercolours by B. Saunders.

At the east end of the High Street, on the south side, stood Castle House. It is likely that an earlier house was given the full Gothic treatment in the early nineteenth century to produce the crenellations and the tower. Originally the house had extensive grounds stretching almost to the site of the present railway line. This view shows the garden front. The house was built flush with the High Street and had no front grounds. Just to the west lay Hackney workhouse, which was rebuilt and expanded after 1841. Castle House became one of Hackney's many private ladies' schools *c.* 1845, run by a Mrs Chrees, and it is likely that the girls in this picture were some of her pupils. The southern part of the grounds were acquired for workhouse expansion in the 1860s. Castle House itself was bought by the Board of Guardians in 1879 to build a new infirmary.

At the end of Homerton High Street. Marsh Hill drops sharply down to the River Lea. This watercolour shows the scene around 1890. On the left the houses at the north end of Sidney (Kenworthy) Road are marked on the Rocque map of 1745, and these may date from the early eighteenth century. Beyond the cyclist the terrace just visible was built *c.* 1886. The curious narrow gabled house may have accommodated the tollhouse keeper. It was demolished *c.* 1897.

After the workhouse extension of 1879, three large houses survived between the workhouse and the junction with Kenworthy Road and are seen here in the late 1880s. Attributed by Clarke to the 1720s, they had lost their back gardens by the 1890s and the pair nearest the infirmary block may have already been in workhouse use. Demolition for further workhouse extensions took place *c.* 1905.

Pratts Lane, *c.* 1870. Before Glyn Road was built, Pratts Lane (named after an eighteenth-century brickmaker) joined the High Street a little to the west of the later Glyn Road junction, and then bent round to the east before following the later Glyn Road alignment. On the left is Healthy Terrace and the back lane to the garden of the Adam and Eve public house. To the right the lane curves round the garden wall of Symington House, and beyond the cottages directly ahead is a glimpse of a Hackney farm, with watercress beds behind it. Watercolour painted from memory by Mr W. Burnett, *c.* 1912.

South end of Marsh House, 1884. This house stood on the north side of Marsh Hill. It had had the extensive grounds of the former Tower Place added to its lands, after the latter was demolished prior to 1870. In the nineteenth century, Marsh House was owned by the Yetts family. It was demolished *c.* 1887. Photograph by Alfred Braddock.

Anyone for tennis? The Beresford family at play in the garden of the White House in 1863. The White House had fishing rights to this part of the River Lea as early as 1810 and the Beresfords were there before 1835. The fishing rights extended further south to a bridge known as the White Bridge, with its adjacent small cottage, also known as the White House. The Beresford house was altered to become a public house in the later nineteenth century, and after losing its licence in 1911 it was demolished in 1917.

TO SOUTH HACKNEY
& HACKNEY WICK

Junction of Lauriston Road and Victoria Park Road, c. 1905. Before development, South Hackney consisted of two small settlements, one around 'Grove Street', the junction of the present Victoria Park Road and Lauriston Road, and the other along Well Street. To the east lay Hackney Wick, which consisted of Wick House and a few cottages in 1745. Here, a horse tram is on its way south. Southborough Road crosses to the north and on the right is a corner of Davis's oil shop, which was to last as a family business until about 1980. There was a local story that the first shop had been destroyed in an explosion during the 1860s while a woman was giving birth, and she was left to her own devices as everyone rushed outside to see what had happened.

From Church Street the way to South Hackney lay through the estate of St Thomas's Hospital. The original Unitarian New Gravel Pit Chapel was built on the west side of Chatham Place in 1809. It was replaced by this Gothic edifice in 1858. This photograph of around 1880 was taken from the field opposite, which was built on in 1861. The New Gravel Pit Chapel closed in 1969 and the building was demolished the following year. The graveyard is still extant beyond a modern block of flats.

Woolpack Place ran south from Morning Lane a little to the west of the junction with Bridge (later Ponsford) Street. The children are standing at the junction with Ribstone Street, in this view looking south. Named either after the Woolpack Inn on Morning Lane (licensed from 1760) and its associated brewery of the same name, Woolpack Place had houses on the east side by 1824. It was designated for slum clearance in 1936 and Woolpack House and Ribstone House had been completed on the site by 1940.

Trinity Chapel, Devonshire (later Brenthouse) Road, *c*. 1900. This chapel stood on the corner with Frampton Park Road. It was built for Congregationalists, who had broken away from the Well Street chapel. It was designed by Matthew Habershon and completed in 1832. It was closed down in 1904. Altered from 1911 to become Devonshire Hall, it was destroyed by bombing in 1940.

Robinson's Retreat was established by Samuel Robinson, who designed the almshouses, with a chapel at the centre, for the widows of Independent and Baptist ministers in 1812. The almshouses were built on the south side of Retreat Place, just west of the Mead Place junction. The plot on the opposite side of Retreat Place was a garden for the almswomen. This watercolour, looking west, includes the tomb of the founder and his wife. Social changes to the area led to the conversion of the almshouses to artisans' dwellings in 1902, and the garden had a factory built on the site. The council later acquired the almshouses and they had been demolished by 1949. The tomb was removed to Abney Park cemetery.

The modern Tudor Road began as a lane to the principal medieval South Hackney house. The western end became Tryon's Place, named after a development built by Thomas Tryon on land he leased in 1696, which was probably completed by 1699. The top view of *c.* 1870 looks toward the western end, where Tryon's Place narrowed to an alley passing through small houses before reaching Mare Street. On the right are two of Tryon's houses, known as Tryon House and Wilton House in 1872. In the 1890s both houses were used by a firm of wholesale milliners, but in 1927 both were in private hands and featured in a women's magazine. Henry Grey, the owner, had built up a substantial collection of antiques. The bottom views show the drawing room and hallway. The house retained oak panelling, which made a fine setting for period furniture, china and tapestries. A factory replaced Tryon House and Wilton House in 1936.

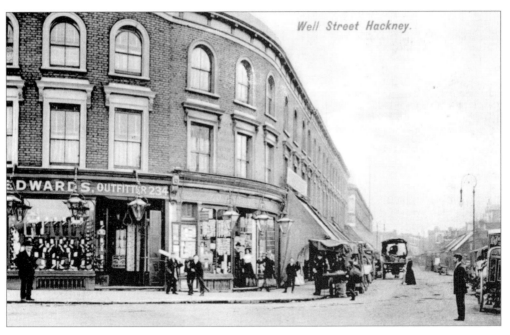

South side of Well Street on the Kenton Road corner, *c*. 1905. Postcard by Charles Martin.

One South Hackney street had a lucky escape in 1941 when this squad was called out to deal with an unexploded landmine. The donor of this photograph could not remember exactly where the mine fell; the houses may be in King Edward Road. Suggestions welcome.

The modern Shore Road was once Shore Place, taking its name from the principal house of the area, which stood on a site behind the present 18 Shore Road. First recorded as De la Grave in 1324, it was rebuilt in brick in 1612, and became a castellated building of five bays. By 1720 the house was in poor repair and, though extended in 1740, it was demolished by the speculator Thomas Flight in 1769. Flight built a later Shore House on part of the garden of the older building.

A very rural scene in Shore Place in the 1820s. The cottages (possibly including a barn) are difficult to locate, but may have been just south of the modern junction of Shore Road and King Edward Road, in which case this view looks west. They would have been demolished when King Edward Road was finally laid out after 1850. Watercolour by C. Bigot.

The Norris family became significant South Hackney landowners in 1653 when Hugh Norris, a city businessman, bought a large house and thirty-one acres. The original house, a rambling Tudor structure with two staircase turrets, possibly dating from the late 1530s, was demolished in 1729 when Henry Norris returned to live on the estate. The top view, a sketch by Toussaint c. 1840, shows the replacement house from Grove Street Lane (the modern Victoria Park Road). It was then the residence of Revd Henry Handley Norris, who was both squire and parson of South Hackney, since he was also the first rector of the newly formed parish after 1825. The bottom plan, a detail from an estate survey of 1803, shows the house and part of the estate, together with the position of the planned second parish church instigated by Norris. After the death of Henry Handley Norris and his widow, the old house was demolished for the development of South Hackney, making way in the early 1860s for Southborough Road.

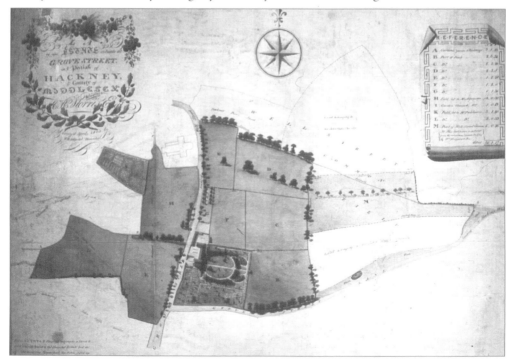

C.J. Greenwood's lithograph of St John of Jerusalem Church probably dates from *c.* 1850. South Hackney's first church, a chapel of ease, was built in Well Street in 1810. Henry Handley Norris was instrumental in securing a new site for the church and in raising funds. The building, designed by E.C. Hakewill, was completed in 1848. The statues and the projecting evangelists' beasts on the tower were removed in the 1880s. The Kentish ragstone was given Speldhurst stone dressings, which was appropriate because Norris had married into the Powell family, whose estate was near Speldhurst. The road layout here was altered in 1862. Greenwood purports to stand in front of Monger's almshouses, looking towards the church and the line of the future King Edward Road.

The rectory of St John of Jerusalem Church, a George James photograph of 1870. Henry Handley Norris had no need of a rectory, and his successors had to make do with houses in the newly created parish until a new rectory was built opposite the church on the corner of Groombridge Road and Grove Street (Lauriston Road in 1860). The building was destroyed by bombing in October 1940. Prideaux house now stands on the site.

Monger's Almshouses were endowed by Henry Monger in his will of 1669 to house six men of more than sixty years of age. They had been completed by the following year on a site on the east side of Grove Street in rural solitude. By 1825, when Robert MacKay made this pencil sketch, they were showing signs of age. They were rebuilt in 1847 (losing the gate and high front wall) and then modernized in 1969. They survive today.

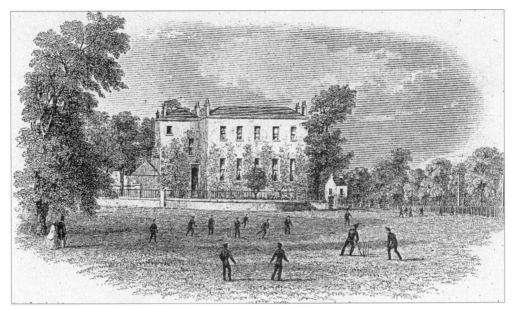

Grove House School. This school occupied the former Common House, which lay just north of Monger's Almshouses and which took its name from Well Street Common. Built in 1787, it became a private boys' school in 1849, taking the new name from an earlier establishment in the old Cass house, or a successor on Grove Street, which had also been called Grove House School. It became a home for deaconesses in 1895 and was demolished when Meynell Gardens was built in 1932.

The Jewish cemetery on the east side of Grove Street (now Lauriston Road) was established in 1786 by members of the Germans' Hambro Synagogue. It was used for burials until 1886. This George James photograph of 1872 shows the lodge, which still survives and the prayer hall which seems to have been demolished once burials ceased. The house on the left is one of the terrace demolished for the building of Ruthven Street and the present shops on the east side of the Broadway in 1872.

The tower of St John of Jerusalem's Church made an imposing end to King Edward Road, as this photograph *c.* 1905 shows. Road alterations in the 1960s broke the street line here and left only the eastern stub of the road (renamed Moulins Road). Changes to the Kingshold Estate will shortly restore the old street line. Three horsedrawn delivery vehicles form a near traffic jam at the end of the road.

The western end of King Edward Road, with the junction with Fremont Street on the right, *c.* 1905. The phaeton is being driven by Dr Henry Dixon, whose surgery was at 134 Mare Street. This end of King Edward Road was first projected in 1842, but only five houses were occupied in 1851.

Captioned by the family, 'The Chief Engineer and staff', Richard Alfred Reader and his three sons, John Thomas (b. 1904), Richard Francis (b. 1903) and Edgar Charles (b. 1905) are proudly displaying their homemade engines in the back garden of 28 Christie Road for Francis Golding's camera in the summer of 1909.

Richard Reader's father-in-law, Francis William Gosling, was a keen amateur photographer who lived nearby at 14 Christie Road. 'Nurse Clara' who attended Mrs Gosling, may have been photographed at no. 14 in 1898.

Edgar Reader painted this view of part of the kitchen of 28 Christie Road in 1940, as it would have appeared in his childhood. Interiors of Hackney houses are comparatively rare, so this gives a delightful glimpse of an Edwardian middle-class house and garden.

Shore Place (now Road) from the corner of King Edward Road, on what must be a Sunday morning, *c.* 1900. The streets are empty of traffic and everyone is dressed in their solemn best. An evocative photograph by Richard Reader.

More or less respectable, this is the Three Colts Tavern which stood at the subsequently south end of Grove Street (now Lauriston Road), with its own tea garden at the rear. This watercolour shows the buildings from Grove Street, *c.* 1830. It was demolished when Victoria Park was under construction in the early 1840s, although the tongue of land on which it stood was subsequently built on in 1874.

St Augustine's Church, South Hackney, lay just inside Victoria Park, opposite Brookfield Road. This postcard dates from *c.* 1900. Designed by J.C. Hakewill and built on a site donated by the Crown in 1867, this church was damaged by bombing in 1944 and demolished *c.* 1952. The site is now marked by a quadrangle of trees.

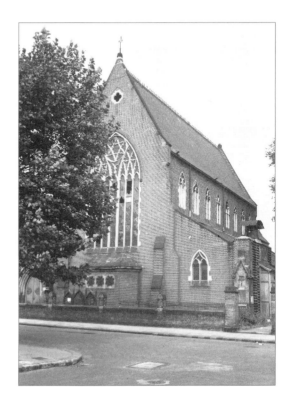

Christ Church, Gore Road stood opposite the junction with Northiam Street in 1944. Designed by W. Wigginton, the church was completed in 1871. Like St Augustine's church it was bomb damaged in 1944. The church had been demolished by 1948 and the parish was combined with that of St John of Jerusalem in 1953. Christ Church Square now occupies part of the site.

Troops stationed at Victoria Park, 1911. In August of this year there was widespread industrial unrest, with strikes in the docks, on the railways and in industry. Part of the government response included transferring regiments from Aldershot to camps in Hackney Marshes and Victoria Park. St Barnabas's Church tower at Homerton was taken over by the military as a signalling post. These and the next two pictures show some of a projected force of 3,000 troops stationed at Victoria Park, including (above) a very small recruit. At least some of the tents were on the east side of Grove Road, where there were football pitches and plenty of open space (see below).

The strikes were ended on Saturday 19 August 1911 and camp must have been struck shortly afterwards.

Bonners Field, open land on the site of the later Victoria Park, was a resort of preachers and radical politicians, and the tradition of soapbox oratory continued with the newly created park of the 1840s. The Burdett Coutts fountain was the principle place for public meetings in the 1890s. This sketch by E.G. Cohen shows a largely male audience listening to rival attractions. Lt-Col. Sexby, author of a history of London parks, was there in 1895 and noted orators from the Social Democratic Federation, the Independent Labour Party, the National Secular Society and various missionary bodies. The Tower Hamlets Mission caused considerable trouble in 1892 when its brass band drowned out the other speakers, and it was only after the entire mission was arrested that its members consented to use a space well away from the fountain.

Sidney House stood on the west side of Sidney Road (Wick Lane in 1830, Kenworthy Road today). It was built by silk manufacturer Leny Smith in 1808–9. Smith went bankrupt and in the early 1830s his house was used as an asylum by a Dr Tuke. Between 1839 and 1841 it was bought by Thomas Ballance, another silk merchant. The top view shows the house from the southern end of Sidney Road in the late 1860s. The bottom view shows a group gathered on the steps of the north front. They are mostly the children of Thomas and Mary Ballance (left to right): Julia Ballance, Mary Eliza Fox, Alfred Charles Ballance, Augusta Ballance, Mary Ballance, George Smart Ballance and Ellen Ballance. Thomas died in 1867, and financial circumstances forced a gradual sale of the estate. Ballance Road was named in 1869 and Hasset Road to the north was under construction in 1871. The house was acquired by a convent and survives today with later additions and alterations.

Victoria Park Station, looking north, *c.* 1905. The original station was at the junction of the North London Railway's Poplar Line and the Great Eastern Line to Stratford. This view shows an NLR 4-4-0 tank with a Bow train crossing over the Gainsborough Road (Eastway) bridge. This station of 1866 replaced an earlier one and closed to all traffic in 1943. All trace was lost when the A102(M) was built through the site in 1970. The present Hackney Wick Station is further to the east on the former GER line.

The White Lion, corner of Bartripp Street and Wick Lane, January 1939. There was a pub here in 1825 with enough ground behind it for the proprietor, John Baum, and his successors to hold boxing competitions and foot races. An exciting race was held here in May 1863 when all comers were invited to challenge Deerfoot, a visiting American Seneca Indian. Sadly, Deerfoot lost, but a row of cottages built at Hackney Wick soon afterwards was named in his honour. Bartripp Street was built over the running grounds in 1876. The site is now part of the motorway slip roads.

Hackney Wick, viewed from a point just north-east of the present bend in Eastway, late 1830s. There have been four phases of development at Hackney Wick, taking the area from outlying farmland through early industrialization, then overlying the area with some of the most badly built slum housing in Hackney, followed by a tower block landscape, which itself has recently been replaced with new housing. This look at Hackney Wick goes back to the second phase, when industry was beginning to creep in among the fields but major development was still twenty-five or so years away. The tall building on the right is part of a ropeworks and is on the site of St Mary at Eton Mission Hall. There is water on the bend in front of the cottage – a reminder of how low-lying the area is. Watercolour by C. Bigot.

Wick Hall, *c.* 1845. Wick Hall stood on the site of the junction of Wick Road and Eastway. The Wick Estate (a 'wick' is an outlying farm) was first recorded in 1185 and there was a hall at the Wick in 1399. The house was rebuilt by John Bayliffe after 1633. The extensive estate was divided in 1763, and it was probably shortly after this that Wick Hall was rebuilt by John Mann (d. 1778). In 1809 the hall was leased to Mark Beaufoy, who made a balloon ascent from there, getting as far as Colchester. From about 1841 it was used as a school kept by Dr and Mrs Eady, and these illustrations appeared in their prospectus issued *c.* 1855, towards the end of the school's existence, which had closed by 1861. Development was then imminent, and Wick Hall and its adjoining buildings had disappeared by the following year.

This 'Gothic' cottage adjoined Wick Hall immediately to the east and its double gables – minus the thatched roof – can just be glimpsed in the top view opposite. Originally the cottage may have been part of the farm range, or even part of the Bayliffe Wick Hall, remodelled as a dower house. This forms part of a series of watercolours of the Hackney Wick area dating from *c.* 1830.

Cadogan Terrace and Riseholme Street were once part of a lane that came up from Old Ford. The home farm for Wick Hall stood on the east side and this watercolour of about 1830 shows the small cottages that stood in front of the main farmyard. The site was redeveloped after 1862 and later became the Eton Manor Boys' Club. Today the motorway crosses this point.

In the 1830s the section of Wick Road between Cassland Road and the Victoria Park Road junction was known as Hackney Wick. This view is described as 'near Hackney Wick' and may be looking west to where Grove Street Lane (later Victoria Park Road) met Wick Lane. The stream on the right is part of the Hackney Brook and the barn may have formed part of one of the many market gardens in the area at the time.

There were two mills in the vicinity of Hackney Wick. Froggatts, built c. 1765, stood north-east of Wick Hall in 1831, a large single-block building that had gone by 1843. Leny Smith's former silk mill of 1787 stood to the south of the site of the Tiger public house on Wick Road; the section of Cassland Road just to the south was then known as Silk Mill Row. This view may show the west end of Smith's mill and associated buildings around 1830. After Smith's failure, the mill was taken by the Children's Friend Society, which was founded by Capt. Edward Brenton to prepare children for emigration to the colonies. The society retained the property until c. 1841. The mills were producing flock and horse hair in the 1840s and the site was redeveloped in 1849, when the present line of Wick Road was created.

DALSTON & VICINITY

This section of the book ranges across the area of Hackney west of Mare Street, including not only Dalston but also the former hamlet of Shacklewell to the north and De Beauvoir Town in the south-west. Before 1830 much of the area between Mare Street and Kingsland Road was farmland. Kingsland – the settlement – lay around what is now Kingsland High Street, and the focus of Dalston was the junction of the present Norfolk Road and Dalston Lane. We begin at Dalston Lane, taken from the Lower Clapton Congregational Chapel in 1884. The view includes Dalston Lane, the Pembury Tavern (built c. 1866) and the Hackney School of Industry. The school started in 1790, taking only girls from 1833, and moved to this building, designed by James Edmeston, in 1837. It closed in 1886 and the building was later acquired by the North East London Institute, the forerunner of Hackney College. The shed in the middle of the road may be temporary accommodation for a nearby livery stable.

Old Dalston Gate, 1845

Dalston Lane gate, looking north towards the site of the present Three Compasses public house, 1845. Maintaining main roads was a considerable burden for local parishes in the eighteenth century, when road traffic was increasing. The solution lay in the creation of turnpike trusts, which took over sections of road, erected gates and charged tolls. The first turnpike road through Hackney was the present A10, which was administered by the Stamford Hill Turnpike Trust from 1713. Hackney Turnpike Trust was established in 1738 for the main road from Cambridge Heath to Stamford Hill via Hackney and Clapton. Dalston Lane was added to the trust's roads in 1799, but had a gate by 1770. Individual turnpike trusts in North London were merged into the Metropolis Road Commission in 1826. The Dalston gate was re-erected in 1839. It stood at the south end of Dalston Lane just north of the present Queensbridge Road junction. The gate was moved again to Navarino Road in 1858, before all gates were abolished in 1864.

The Manor House, Dalston Lane. This house dated from the early nineteenth-century and was on the site of a seventeenth-century house owned by the Blackall family. It was never a real manor house. In 1849 it was acquired by the Refuge for the Destitute, which was founded in 1805 to provide a home for discharged prisoners and other unfortunates. The refuge had two premises in Shoreditch (from 1811 on the Hackney Road for women and from 1815 at the bottom of Hoxton Street for men). All the government grant was withdrawn by 1849 and this prompted a rethink: both of the Shoreditch premises were closed, while the refuge ceased to take in men and moved its women's home to Dalston. These two photographs are from the centenary appeal and show the front of the house and the kitchen (with inmates). The refuge merged with the Elizabeth Fry Refuge in 1923 and the Manor House was then closed. Samuel Lewis Trust flats were built on the site in 1924.

Dalston Infant Asylum. The house opposite the Manor House was taken over by the Dalston Infant Asylum in 1832, which had been founded five years before. The top view shows the house and its outbuildings as drawn by George Hawkins in 1836. There were 170 children here in three properties by 1842 and the asylum moved out to Wanstead in the following year. Its place was taken by the German Hospital, which opened in 1845 and catered for Germans and German speakers. The bottom view, a lithograph of 1846, shows the rear of the Dalston Lane buildings. These were demolished when a new building was built further to the south in 1864 and the original site was let for new building. The German Hospital closed in 1987.

Dalston Lane, looking east from Dalston Junction towards the Ashwin Street junction and the Railway Tavern (built 1868), 1905. The pub had become a betting shop by the early 1970s.

New Year's Day party, Clifton Lodge Day Nursery, 96 Dalston Lane, 1944. Day nurseries were established well before the Second World War, but the need for day care for children increased as more and more women were included in the workforce.

Shacklewell was a small settlement along a lane that included part of what is now Rectory Road, both parts forming a loop from Dalston to Stoke Newington. One of Hackney's richest men in the early sixteenth century, Sir John Heron, had an estate in this area of the parish, and his house stood on the north side of Shacklewell Lane. It was sold to Alderman Thomas Rowe by Heron's son in 1566 and remained in the Rowe family until they in turn sold the estate to Francis Tyssen in 1685. Both Francis (d.1710) and his son, also Francis (d. 1717), lived here and, as they had acquired both of the major Hackney manors, the house became the Manor House. The engraving shows the house as it would have appeared in the 1720s. The old house had been demolished by 1762, and twelve new houses were erected on the site, north-west of Shacklewell Green.

The Manor House, Shacklewell Green, 1870. One of the new houses on the north side of Shacklewell Green succeeded to the title of the Manor House. This view shows the fine gateposts and the house, though regrettably the photographer has not included the immediate surroundings. A gardener can be seen through the gateway, resting on his barrow. The old house appears to have been extended after 1820, and the exterior, remarkably similar to the house built for J.R.D. Tyssen on Church Street (later Mare Street) in 1845 suggests that this house was either rebuilt or refronted at around the same date. The Manor House was leased in the 1840s and survived until the construction of Seal Street on the site *c.* 1880.

Shacklewell, looking north across the north end of the Green, April 1885. The seclusion of Shacklewell began to disappear in the 1880s and has now been lost so completely that it is hard to imagine that it was once a rural hamlet. The open space on the left was cleared as part of the construction of Perch Street, which began in 1883.

The top end of Norfolk (now Cecilia) Road, April 1885. This photograph shows the row of houses built on the site of the old manor house in the 1760s. (on the same day as the top view), victims of clearance by Hackney Council in 1936.

Cecilia Road was built on the line of Love Lane, a footpath and track running north from Dalston to Shacklewell. This watercolour by C.H. Matthews of 1850, was drawn from a point near the present junction with Colvestone Crescent. The path maintains its original level – land either side had been dug out for brick earth. On the right, flying a tricolour, is Betty Harcombe's cottage, which Hackney's first town clerk, George Grocott, recalled as his schoolboy tuck shop in the 1850s. Beyond are the backs of the houses on the south side of Shacklewell Green.

Front of Betty Harcombe's cottage, from across Love Lane, *c.* 1860. The cottage and footpath vanished in 1862 when Norfolk Road (today's Cecilia Road), was constructed.

The Lock Hospital. The junction of Kingsland Road and Balls Pond Road was another of Hackney's tollgate sites, but here was to be found Hackney's oldest hospital. The top view shows the Balls Pond Road frontage. The tollgate was put up by the Stamford Hill Turnpike Trust and existed from 1713 to 1864. On the left is St Bartholomew's Chapel, which was built to serve the Lock Hospital, the roof of which is just visible behind it. The building on the far left on Kingsland Road housed an auctioneer in the 1830s and still exists, behind shops, today. The bottom view shows the Kingsland Road elevation. The Lock Hospital (far left) was founded *c.* 1280 and was run by St Bartholomew's Hospital from 1549. It was intended for lepers, but all those with skin diseases were cared for by an official called the Guide. The hospital premises were rebuilt from 1723 to 1727. Rising costs brought about its closure in 1760. Both views were drawn in the 1850s but depict the scene of thirty or so years before.

Interior of Kingsland or St Bartholomew's Chapel, looking towards the east window, early 1830s. This tiny chapel continued as a chapel of ease for local people after the hospital was closed. The minister was nominated by the governors of St Bartholomew's Hospital, though financial support came from the congregation. This watercolour by George Hawkins, probably done in the early 1850s, shows the interior of the tiny chapel, which was bisected by the Hackney–Islington parish boundary. Hawkins was facing the east window and was standing three feet below the outside ground level. The space inside is crammed with box and gallery pews, and the pulpit is just visible to the left. The chapel served local people as well as inmates, though in 1716 a disturbance caused by outsiders resulted in the provision of curtains to keep the patients out of sight. By 1842 the congregation had shrunk to twenty and the chapel finally closed in 1845. Sadly the building was demolished and a public house (now a betting shop) was built on the site.

Remains of abandoned conduit, 1852. Under an Act of 1543 the City of London was authorized to draw water from a number of places outside its bounds, including Hackney. However, a chalybeate spring between Church (Mare) Street and Dalston was being used in 1535, after Londoners had voted for funds to construct pipes to Aldgate. The head was near the later Navarino Road. The abandoned conduit may have been on the east side of the road, just south of where the road crosses the present North London Line. An inspection in 1692 confirmed that the water was still plentiful, but that locals had damaged the doors and stolen lead fittings. Ruin had set in by 1852, but the remains of the coat of arms of the City were still visible, as well as a quantity of ancient graffiti. In its last days the conduit house nearby was used as a tool store for Smith's nursery.

Kingsland Green, to the north-west of the Kingsland Road and Balls Pond Road junction, is bisected by the Hackney–Islington boundary. In the 1870s it was privately owned, but still open on the east side. On the west there was a row of early eighteenth-century houses. The top view shows two of these from 1875. By this date most of the Green was used as a plant nursery. In 1880 there was an attempt to buy the Green and make it a public open space, but the asking price was too high. In 1882 the houses on the west side were demolished and the Green was obliterated. The bottom view, looking south to Kingsland Passage, shows the shops and buildings that resulted. Those to the left have in turn been replaced, and the site of those facing is now a small car park.

Heavy horse traffic on Kingsland Road, alongside Kingsland Crescent, looking south from the Englefield Road junction. A watercolour by C.H. Matthews of about 1850 but harking back to an earlier period. Kingsland Crescent was one of a number of late eighteenth- and early nineteenth-century developments on Kingsland Road, and it was under construction in 1793. The Fox, alongside, was rebuilt in 1790, in front of an earlier alehouse of the same name.

Further down Kingsland Road, looking north, this view of *c.* 1905 shows the impressive fire station built in 1895 on the left. This replaced an earlier station in St Peter's Road. A new fire station replaced this building in 1977. Beyond is the Metropolitan Free Hospital, which was founded in 1836 and moved to this newly constructed building in 1885. The hospital closed in 1977 and now houses a variety of

Another C.H. Matthews' watercolour illustrating an eighteenth-century scene, but probably showing part of the de Beauvoir estate, *c.* 1830. Mr Fox, the gentleman in the black hat, who is on his way home to dinner, is walking along a path on the approximate line of the modern Hertford Road. To his right is a small market garden, and to the left the brickfields of William Rhodes, who had secured a substantial building lease from estate owner Peter de Beauvoir in 1821. This was to lead to legal action with de Beauvoir's heir, Richard Benyon de Beauvoir – a case that Rhodes lost. Brickmaking was common in Hackney, but pictures that record it are comparatively rare. On the far right are houses on the east side of Kingsland Road.

Balmes or Whitmore House, from the south side of the Regent's Canal, a C.H. Matthews' watercolour of *c.* 1850. The canal had been completed through Hackney in 1820. The bridge (right) was originally provided for the private drive to Whitmore House. In this form the house dated back to a substantial rebuilding carried out by Sir George Whitmore in 1635. The De Beauvoir family acquired the estate in 1687 but later moved to a house at Downham in Essex. Whitmore House was then let and from 1756 was used as an asylum.

Balmes House. Balmes probably derives its name from Adam Bamme (d. 1397), a mayor of London, whose estate included the reputed Hoxton Manor, the principal seat of which was on the site of the later Balmes House or Whitmore House. In the seventeenth century the house was set in formal gardens, with a home farm on the site of the east side of the bottom end of De Beauvoir Road. There were two small structures on the west wall of the estate, and this may have been the most northerly of the two, on a site lost under the modern council estate south of Downham Road.

The south side of Balme's house, a drawing by Robert Schnebbelie 18 September 1816. By this time the house, now an asylum, was being run by Thomas Warburton, who was said to operate a brutal regime. A parliamentary enquiry into conditions in asylums in 1815 included extensive reports into Warburton's establishments, including Whitmore's, and some improvements resulted. It was the development of the De Beauvoir estate after the conclusion of the legal battle with Rhodes that sealed the fate of Whitmore House. The asylum closed in 1851 and the line of Whitmore Road was extended, as De Beauvoir Road, through the site.

Richmond Road, from the junction with Queens (now Queensbridge) Road, *c.* 1905. Richmond Road was one of the first streets built on the Lamb Farm estate in about 1830, running just north of Swan Lane (first Grange and then Lenthall Road), which led to Lamb Farm. The developers were William and Thomas Rhodes. William had been responsible for the initial development of De Beauvoir Town. The spire (left) belonged to St Philip's Church, the site of which was given by William Rhodes. The church, designed by Henry Duesbury, was completed in 1841. It was bombed in 1940 and had been demolished by 1952.

Dalston Wesleyan Church, corner of Richmond Road and Mayfield Road, looking north-west, April 1883. The church was built in 1865 for a congregation that had formerly worshipped in Roseberry Place. Bomb damaged in 1945, it was rebuilt as a mission church in 1961.

Before the Second World War, Eleanor Road extended south of its present stump to meet Tower (now Martello) Street by the junction with London Lane. On the west side there was a large Board school, which was completed in 1898. All of this was to change after the night of 21/22 September 1940, when the area was heavily bombed. These photographs, the only ones to survive among the official records kept by the

metropolitan borough of Hackney, show the results. The school, which was burned out, did not reopen. After the war it was decided to clear the whole area, including houses on the west side of Tower Street, so today the sole survivor is the Queen Eleanor public house and it is hard to imagine that this area was ever anything other than part of London Fields. The images on these two pages are taken from a single panoramic view.

The east side of London Fields, just south of the bend eastwards in Tower Street, *c.* 1910. Directly ahead is Arnold House, which was substantially rebuilt from an earlier house in 1825. It was altered again, being divided into two houses probably at the time that a terrace was built in the back garden in 1858. Arnold House was almost certainly damaged in the September 1940 bombing and was later demolished.

Looking across the Cat and Mutton Bridge at the bottom end of Broadway Market, just inside the Shoreditch boundary in 1905. This could be another Sunday morning view, this time in a very poor district. On the right is St Stephen's Church, serving a parish that was formed in 1864. Built shortly after 1872, the church was damaged in the Blitz, which also destroyed many of the adjoining houses. After the war a small part of the church was repaired, but it was finally closed in 1953. Debdale House now stands on the site.

CLAPTON &
LEA BRIDGE

Clapton takes its name from the Old English for 'the farm on the hill', possibly a reference to a farmstead that stood at the top of the high ground rising from the River Lea. It came to be applied to the whole north-eastern area of the parish, with an approximate division into Upper and Lower on the line of Lea Bridge Road. This section concentrates on Lower Clapton, but also includes Hackney Downs, Lea Bridge and a little of the River Lea itself. Lower Clapton Road starts at the top end of Mare Street; this first view of 1898 shows a pair of houses on the corner of the new churchyard, built at the end of Portland Place after the rest of the terrace had been completed in the early 1830s. In use as a YMCA hostel for women, the houses were replaced by a police station in 1904.

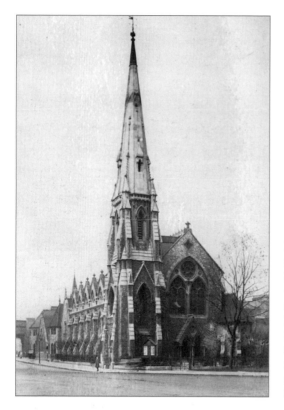

Lower Clapton Congregational Church, corner of Pembury Road and Amhurst Road, c. 1905. Designed by Henry Fuller in 1864, this church was built for the congregation that had broken away from St Thomas Square Chapel, and had leased a small chapel on the north side of Pembury Grove in 1850. The new church remained in use until 1936, when the congregation moved to the former Presbyterian church on the corner of Cricketfield Road. Downs Court flats now occupy the site.

Lower Clapton Congregational Church provided a splendid end to this part of Amhurst Road, as this George James view in a summer around 1870, demonstrates.

A cold winter walk on Hackney Downs, near the north end of Queensdown Road, *c.* 1890. The houses at this end were built in 1869 and no. 2 had become Downs College in 1890. Downs Park Baptist Chapel, at the end of the row, was built in 1868–9 and designed by Morton E. Glover. Photograph by Alfred Braddock.

Cricketfield Road, looking north from the Queensdown Road junction, in a postcard view of *c.* 1910. James Girling's stables are on the left. The road was laid out *c.* 1865 and the houses on the left were built in 1868.

Clapton Square, west side, *c.* 1905. Clapton Square was laid out in 1816, and the houses on the west side were occupied by the following year, when residents included the manorial steward, Thomas Tebbutt. The gardens in the centre of the square were originally for residents only, but after a period of neglect they were acquired by London County Council in 1924 and handed over to Hackney Metropolitan Borough, the successor of which, the London Borough of Hackney, continues to care for them today.

Clapton Square, north-east corner, 1891. The west side has remained substantially unchanged, but there have been considerable alterations to the east. To the left of the two houses at the north-east corner of the square is Clapton Passage. These houses were both built after 1816 and were demolished for the construction of St John's Mansions in 1901.

Hackney Church of England Grammar School was founded as a riposte to the Hackney Proprietary Grammar School in Sutton Place, and it opened on the west side of Clarence Road in 1830. This George Hawkins watercolour of 1836 was drawn from the north-west end of Clapton Square. The building was designed by William MacIntosh Brookes. The Doric portico must have made the building more expensive than its rival. There was a connection with King's College, London, from the inception. The school took boarders, and also had places for day boys, including Benjamin Clarke, who left a vivid recollection of a schoolboy battle in Hackney Churchyard when the boys of the two grammar schools combined against the Free and Parochial School. Merged with the Proprietary School before 1848, the Grammar School needed to be rescued from debt c. 1880, but it lasted for a further fifteen years. A soft drinks factory took over the building until 1903, when it was demolished for Clarence Gardens Flats, which in turn have made way for a road on the Pembury Estate.

Hackney School was founded by Benjamin Morland in 1685 and was passed to his son-in-law Henry Newcome, probably *c.* 1721. It became the most celebrated of all Hackney's private schools. This view of *c.* 1810 shows the rear of the double-gabled house on the east side of Lower Clapton Road. Leading Whig grandees sent their sons here, including the Cavendishs and the children of the 2nd Earl of Hardwicke. The school became famous for its plays. One of those contributing a prologue was actor David Garrick in 1763. The school was administered by successive generations of the Newcome family until 1803. It closed in 1815.

Errata

Page 22 (bottom)

Caption should read: 'George James has caught the attention of some of Matthew Rose's potential customers in this view of around 1872. Dennis' grocery is on the right. The tall block on the left, which included The Three Cranes Public house, had already been rebuilt by 1870; the shops to the south were all demolished between 1877 and 1879, when the Metropolitan Board of Works met the cost of widening this part of the road.'

Page 76 (top)

Fourth sentence should read: 'This photograph of around 1860 . . .'

Page 112 (bottom)

The last sentence should read: 'The hospital closed in 1977 and now houses a variety of workshops.'

Page 145 (bottom)

The last sentence should read: 'The firm left Hackney c. 1960.'

This small group of shops were part of the west side of Lower Clapton Road in 1890. At this time the shops were not numbered, though they subsequently became nos 137–143. A narrow passageway led through Lewis's decorator's premises to a yard at the back. Alongside is William Billet's bootmaker's shop, and the other small building on the right houses Miss Cushing's sweet shop. Originally this would have served Priory House School, which occupied the building just visible behind it. This was founded in 1850 by Samuel Prout Newcombe, who took the name from an earlier establishment that he had run in Islington. Run by Howard Anderton from 1857 to 1886, the school moved to Upper Clapton. After a brief period as a private girls' school, Priory House became a hearth rug factory. All of the buildings in this view were demolished *c.* 1909 to build a skating rink.

(*Opposite, bottom*) The extensive site of Hackney School made it an ideal site for the newly formed London Orphan Asylum, which acquired the property in 1819 and swept away the old school buildings to build new premises. George Hawkins recorded the finished building from the bustle of Lower Clapton Road in 1826, dedicating this engraving to the Asylum's patrons and officials. The asylum was founded in 1813 by Andrew Reed, and provided a boys and girls school with a central chapel. There were 206 children in 1826, rising to 453 in the 1860s. The asylum closed in 1871 and was then briefly occupied by the Metropolitan Asylum Board from 1873 to 1876, before the estate was broken up for building and the Salvation Army acquired the buildings as new headquarters in 1882, carrying out substantial alterations. After the Salvation Army left in 1970, all but the central portico, standing at the end of Linscott Road, was demolished. Painting by George Hawkins.

Hackney House, completed by 1732, included a large estate on the east side of Lower Clapton Road. When the house and its estate were sold in 1786, much was acquired by Hackney College. When that in turn closed in 1799, the house was demolished and the estate divided. There were already a number of houses between Lower Clapton Road and the boundary of the estate, known as the Five Houses, which dated back to the early eighteenth century. The middle house, bought by Benjamin Boddington in 1785, was sold in 1822 to William Amory, who demolished it and built a new house further back from the road. This was The Hall. It had a central Ionic pediment and was drawn on a plan of 1860. It was sold to John Berger, of the paint-making family, in 1830. The bottom view, from the same plan, shows part of the estate, taken from the grounds of the former Hackney House, all of which was acquired for redevelopment in 1861 by the London and Suburban Land and Property Company.

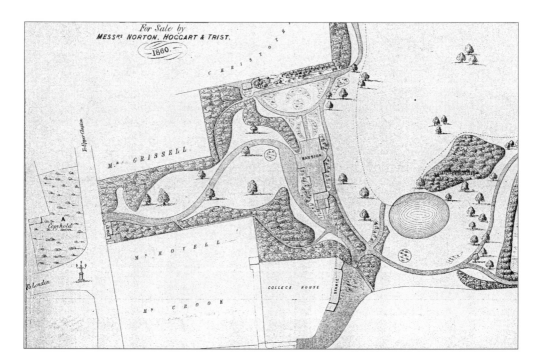

The Priory stood further back in the park and probably dated from the early 1820s. It stood near the present junction of Dunlace Road and Elderfield Road, and it may have served as a dower house for the Amory family. Demolished when the estate was broken up, it is commemorated today in the Priory Tavern.

The Nyren family in the back garden of College House, late 1870s. The position of College House can be seen from the adjoining plan. It was built on the former stable yard of Hackney House for the resident Hackney College tutor, Abraham Rees, soon after 1785. The Nyrens lived here from 1870, and Elizabeth, the youngest daughter, recalled the lovely arbutus trees and the powerfully scented lilacs. College House was demolished c. 1883 for the construction of the now vanished Lesbia Road. Later excavations revealed that the cellars had survived the demolition. Their layout suggests that they may have belonged to a much earlier house that may have preceded Cole Campbell's Hackney House of 1732.

Glyn Road Mission Hall was at the north end of Lower Clapton Road at the junction with Pressburg Street and was photographed around 1900. Run by Clapton Park Congregational Church and opened in 1882, the hall had a school alongside. The mission was closed in 1939 and the building served briefly as a warehouse, before being bombed and later demolished.

Clapton Park Tabernacle. The tabernacle stood on the south side of Blurton Road, just west of the junction with Chatsworth Road and this view from Chatsworth Road was taken around 1900. Beginning as a Primitive Methodist mission in the former Theatre Royal, Glenarm Road, this building was completed in 1885. Damaged in the Second World War, the mission was replaced by the present church in Chatsworth Road in 1958. The former tabernacle later served as St Jude's Roman Catholic Church from 1965.

A knees-up is just about to start to get the Pedro Street celebrations of the Jubilee of the reign of George V, 1935 well under way.

This is the west end of Powerscroft Road as captured by Alfred Braddock in 1900. No one would risk a bicycle in such a position now. On the right is the Sunday School of Clapton Park Congregational Church, which today serves the congregation as a place of worship. The adjoining Round Chapel was designed by Henry Fuller and completed in 1871 for a group that broke away from Ram's Episcopal Chapel. After a period of considerable uncertainty, the church is to be restored and used for the performing arts, in conjunction with continued worship in the former Sunday School. Powerscroft Road was created by the London and Suburban Land and Building Company in 1867.

The Elms, east side of Clapton Pond, in the course of demolition, 1890. This house was one of a pair built in the early eighteenth century. Its northern neighbour was the home of a wealthy member of Hackney's Jewish community, Joshua Israel Brandon, whose garden included an ornamental canal and a Chinese summer house on his death in 1772. In 1844 the Elms was taken over by William and Mary Hewitt, whose literary visitors included Mrs Gaskell. Newick Road and St James Villas were built on the site of the Elms and its neighbours to the north.

One of the few scenes in this book that will be familiar today. Taken in April 1900, it shows the southern end of Bishop Wood's Almshouses, founded in 1635 by Thomas Wood, Bishop of Lichfield (whose family lived in Clapton House to the north of Clapton Pond). Intended for ten widows, they were taken over by Hackney parish in 1798 after a dispute with the Powell family, who had acquired the remainder of the Wood Estate, including Clapton Pond. The wings of the almshouses had two tenements, each originally having a single room. After restoration in 1930, the space for inmates was extended. The chapel in the centre is claimed to be the smallest in Britain.

This house was formerly on the west side of Clapton Pond and was built in the early eighteenth century. The extensive grounds reached back to Downs (once Love) Lane and included farm buildings on the site of the junction of Powell Road and Heyworth Road. In 1810 the property was bought by John Clark Powell, whose family owned a substantial estate in Hackney, including Clapton Pond. Powell died there in 1847. After the death of the last of his sisters in 1861, the houses and estate were sold, and Powell Road, Heyworth Road and Charnock Road were laid out. Photograph of c. 1860.

The site of the house was acquired for Clapton Wesleyan Church, completed between 1863 and 1865, and seating 1,000. This view across Clapton Pond, taken in July 1900, shows the church, and in the distance the spire of St James Church. Declining numbers prompted the closure of Clapton Wesleyan Church in 1934, and it was then demolished. The former school, built in Downs Park Road around 1880, became the church, and remains a place of worship today.

Clapton Gate, *c.* 1830. A spot of fast driving was needed if the tollgate was to be avoided. The Clapton gate stood on a site in what is now the middle of the Lea Bridge roundabout and this drawing includes the houses on the site of the Kenninghall Road junction. The gate was installed by the Hackney Turnpike Trust shortly after 1758, when Lea Bridge was built and the road improved by the Lea Bridge and Road Trust. Stagecoaches used this route to bring in businessmen who lived in Leyton and Walthamstow to the City of London, but after the construction of the railway in 1840 the majority of traffic was light carriages carrying people out to Epping Forest. Use of the road increased in the 1850s and at last public pressure secured the abolition of the gate in 1856.

These weatherboarded cottages stood on the north side of Pond Lane (now Millfields Road), behind Bow House, facing onto Clapton Pond. These cottages were already under threat when Alfred Braddock took this view in 1888, and recognized as a survival from Hackney's village but they were demolished in 1896.

Barges unload at Middlesex Wharf on the west side of the River Lea, *c.* 1870. The second bridge of 1820–1 is in the distance. When George James took this view the businesses on the wharf included a boat builder and Davies & Co.'s slate and marble concern. Beyond the bridge the chimney forms part of the East London Waterworks. Parts of the wharf were bombed and the last house by the bridge disappeared shortly after 1950.

Two views of the area now covered by Lea Bridge roundabout. The top one of 1905 shows the lamp and bollards on the site of the former tollgate. Behind the gas light is one of Hackney's new electric streetlights, which were installed shortly after 1900. The houses on the left were built in 1880. The bottom view of 1913 shows the row on the north side of Lea Bridge Road, with a good crowd outside the fishmonger's shop established by John Ockleford. This row was demolished shortly afterwards as part of a road-widening scheme. It was replaced by a smaller row, set further back.

The Jolly Anglers public house was on the west side of the River Lea, just south of the footpath that descends from Southwold Road, 1800. This view looks north from what later became Middlesex Wharf. Between 1830 and 1843 the river frontage here was altered and the pub was rebuilt. The new premises remained in use as a pub until *c.* 1908. Thereafter they appear to have been used for industrial purposes and had been demolished by 1950.

Looking south from Lea Bridge, *c.* 1830. Lea Bridge mills straddled a branch of the River Lea onto an island. There was a mill in this vicinity in the fourteenth century, giving its name to North and South Mill fields. Waterworks were established north of the bridge between 1707 and 1709 by Francis Tyssen. These failed in 1762 and new works were established south of the bridge, which included mill buildings, used to produce flour.

The Lea Bridge Mill burned down in 1796, but was rebuilt. Both mill and waterworks were bought by the East London Waterworks Company in 1832 and had been demolished by the autumn of the following year. This watercolour of the late 1800s by C. Bigot, shows the mill from the south. Engine gear for the original waterworks would have been on the left of the mill, fed by a separate channel. There was formerly a lock on the branch of the River Lea in front of the mill. On the right bank is the Horse and Groom public house.

The Horse and Groom public house, seen from the landward side, late 1820s. In 1762 this was Chevaliers Ferry House. In 1821 the pub still retained a fishery and had its own gardens. By 1848 it was run by the Beresford family. The pub was still trading in 1855, but had closed by 1860 and the site was taken for further waterworks buildings shortly after 1868.

THE WORLD OF WORK

The Hackney muster of lamp lighters from the Gas Light and Coke Company have gathered round their gaffer and his dog at the end of Paragon Road, October 1906. In the days of streetlighting by gas there was no automatic ignition and lamp lighters were needed each night, and each morning to extinguish the lamps. Industrial activity in Hackney can be traced back to the 1530s, when the names of crofts suggest that brickmaking and gravel extraction were already in progress. Silk weavers were recorded in the parish in 1609. The Hackney Brook and the River Lea provided sources of water power, and at Temple Mills there was a leather mill before 1593, which had switched to gunpowder in the early seventeenth century. The same premises may have been used for gun metal made to a special formula for Prince Rupert, the secret of which died with him in 1682. The first factories in the modern sense can be traced back to the mid-eighteenth century and, although Hackney's development was primarily residential, Hackney Wick, the River Lea and the Regents Canal all provided attractive industrial sites. This section looks at a small part of Hackney's varied business world.

Lewis Berger had emigrated from Hanover in Germany in the 1750s. Initially settling in Shadwell, he established a small works making colours. Seeking space to expand, he rented a farmhouse and land at Homerton between Morning Lane and Shepherd Lane, alongside the Hackney Brook. He rebuilt the farmhouse as his residence. The top view shows the frontage onto Shepherds Lane. The bottom view is from the garden. Both photographs were taken for the 150th anniversary history of the Company, which was published in 1910.

Lewis Berger died in 1814 and the business passed to his sons, Samuel (d. 1855) and John (d. 1860), who moved from the business site and bought an adjacent estate, which included two of the Five Houses (see page 126). John's sons Capel Berrow and Lewis Curwood Berger also came into the business and expanded from colours into paint manufacture. Bergers became a limited company in 1879. Two large warehouses and factory buildings were constructed, one alongside the old house on Shepherds Lane and the other at the southern end of the site at the junction of Morning Lane and what is now Berger Road. Even so, much of the site remained very green and open as this photograph of around 1870 shows. Taken from an entrance near the site of Hackney Council's Social Services office (itself a former Berger building), it includes 'the dairy' on the right and the main warehouse ahead.

The top view, of *c.* 1870, was taken looking north from roughly level with the back of the old house. The clock tower was put up before 1810 and survived on top of later factory buildings until the end. The arm of a weighing machine is just visible over the hedge. Ahead is part of the North London Railway viaduct, which cut through the northern part of the site in 1850 and was later to provide considerable storage space under its arches. The lower view shows the ornamental water that lay behind the old house and the clock tower to the north. The Hackney Brook, which formerly flowed through the site, had been culverted by this date.

In common with other employers of the day, Bergers had many employees who worked for the company for life and families who had one or more generations employed there. This view shows an unnamed stalwart, possibly in one of the packing areas, in about 1870.

A convention of Berger travelling salesmen at the back of the old house, *c.* 1907. The last family member to run the company, Arthur Berger, put the firm's money into unwise ventures and speculated on his own account. By 1894 he had brought the firm to the brink of disaster. The manager, John Garson, took control after Arthur Berger was ousted in a boardroom coup, and eventually succeeded in persuading the American company Sherwin Williams to take Bergers over. Garson stayed on and new vitality was injected into the company. Reinvested British capital made Bergers a British firm again by 1914. Manufacture ceased at the Homerton site in 1960, bringing Hackney's 180-year-old paint-making industry to an end. Bergers was taken over and the name subsumed into the Crown Group in the late 1980s.

Hackney was also one of the cradles of the modern British petrochemical industry. Eugene Carless established his distilling and oil refining business in 1859 on land adjoining White Post Lane, and built the Hope Chemical Works. In the 1860s, Carless became the leading distillery in Britain for the newly imported American crude oil, and it pioneered the production of benzoline and paraffin oil. A brief partnership with George Capel was dissolved, leaving only the name. A later partnership with John Hare Leonard, who injected fresh capital, created the business of Carless Capel and Leonard. In 1895, Leonard expanded to acquire the adjoining Pharos works and began to import a range of products, including petroleum. An associate of motor pioneer Gottlieb Daimler, Frederick Simms, suggested that a new tradename should be coined for what was then called 'motor spirit', and thus the tradename 'petrol' was born. Carless Capel and Leonard supplied the new fuel to cars taking part in the famous Emancipation Run to Brighton in 1893, and at the turn of the century Carless Petrol was virtually the only British highly refined motor spirit on the market. This view shows part of the Hope works in about 1950 with distilled spirit canisters being loaded into an open lorry. The firm expanded again to acquire the Lea Works in 1907. Bombing interrupted, but did not halt, production during the Second World War, and Hackney Wick only ceased to be a manufacturing point in 1970. Carless Capel and Leonard became a public company the following year, seeking capital to expand into North Sea gas concentrate refining. The Hackney Wick connection finally ended in 1984. Although taken over in 1989, part of the old company survives as a subsidiary of Repsol, based in Romford.

Tentmaking, *c.* 1910. Thomas Briggs had a tentmaking factory at the south end of Southgate Road by the Regent's Canal on the site of an earlier factory (built by 1823). Briggs's building survives today, divided into workshops.

The finishing shop of Frank & Co.'s works, Silesia Buildings, 215 Mare Street, *c.* 1920. The shoe trade in Hackney was concentrated south and south-east of London Fields from 1880 onwards. By the late 1930s the London footwear industry was centred in Hackney and it remained so until the 1960s. There is still a considerable specialist shoe trade around Well Street today.

Marconi's Wireless Telegraph Company established their extensive works in Tyssen Street, Dalston around 1905 and this view shows the newly completed building. Other specialist engineering firms in Hackney included Tyer & Co., inventors of a railway signalling system, in Ashwin Street until the 1960s, Nalder Bros & Thompson, makers of electrical measuring instruments in Dalston Lane from 1899 to *c.* 1969, and Siemen Bros, which had a lamp factory in Tyssen Street from 1908 to 1923. The Mentmore Manufacturing Company started in 1921 in Mentmore Terrace, moving to Tudor Grove in 1923, where in 1948 it claimed to be Europe's largest fountain pen maker from the Platignum House factory.

It was not all work. This horse brake excursion from the Paget Arms, Middleton Road, may be a works or club outing and is ready for the off in 1905.

W.A. Chardin's printing business set up in a little wooden shop, with a good display of engravings, *c.* 1880. Hackney shops are recorded in Church Street (Mare Street) from the mid-eighteenth century, and there were a number of small buildings put up in the front gardens of former houses by the mid-nineteenth century. Chardin's business was established in the 1860s on what was to become 235 Lower Clapton Road, just north of the White Hart public house.

The River Lea made a good location for some of Hackney's more noxious industrial activity. J.C. Ingram established a small factory in Wilmer Gardens, Hoxton, in 1847, making toy balloons. He was one of the pioneers of rubber surgical goods, and his activity soon outgrew the cramped Hoxton site. In 1866 he acquired land on the east side of Chapman Road and constructed a works after 1872. This engraving shows the works from the west end with Felstead Road on the left. The curve of the railway line has been made much sharper than it was in reality. Ingram's works were bombed in the war and maintained production in the open air for a while. The firm left

Clarke Nickolls and Coombs, confectionery and jam makers were founded in 1872 and by 1879 had established a factory on the west bank of the Hackney Cut north of Carpenters Road. In the 1930s it claimed to be the largest general confectionery maker in Britain. In the 1890s the business expanded to the east bank of the cut, and by 1899 it had taken over an old tar and chemical works south of the railway. The top view of *c.* 1896–8 shows the liquorice, crystallizing and packing works north of the Great Eastern railway bridge. The bottom view of the same date shows the chocolate department, storage areas and yards with the fire station.

Clarke Nickolls and Coombs, loading yard north of the factory, looking east, *c.* 1896–8. Directly ahead is part of the sugar mill. The buildings at the top left are part of the Falcon Chemical works.

Clarke Nickolls and Coombs workforce, Wallis Road, with the factory on the right at lunchtime, 1890s. This company was one of the largest employers in Hackney at this time. The majority of the workforce were women, employed in manufacture and packing. The company provided its own dining rooms and introduced a profit-sharing scheme in 1890. Other social benefits included a provident club, numerous social clubs and a convalescence guest house at Clacton.

Two groups of workers from Clarke Nickolls and Coombs. The top view shows staff from an unidentified department in a street near the factory, *c.* 1905. The bottom view shows staff from the fire department with fire buckets and extinguishers. The company later developed its own portable chemical fire extinguisher (the No. 1 Fire Demon), which was on sale for 30*s* in 1906 for domestic, factory or car use.

The higher echelons of power at Clarke Nickolls and Coombs, 1905. This is the managing director's office. Hard thinking on future business strategy is in progress. The company changed its registered name to Clarnico in 1946, the name that had long been associated with its products.

The Clarke Nickolls and Coombs factory display room. By the turn of the century the company was making a variety of chocolates, fondants, marzipan, sweet cigarettes, caramels and fruits. Fancy packaging ranged from drums and teapots, to toy engines, horns, yachts and violins. The factory was badly bombed in 1944 and production of many items was still curtailed after the new works in Waterden Road were completed in 1955. However, Clarnico's was able to meet the demand for its famous Mitcham Mints.

The Clarnico's fire brigade's own horsedrawn steamer, all ready for a run in 1904. The fire station was later moved to the new works on the east side of the Hackney Cut. This photograph may have been taken in Kings Yard, just north of Carpenters Road. The fire brigade visited Boulogne, Paris and Brussels on annual trips between 1903 and 1905.

Improvised hospital set up inside Clarnico's works, *c.* 1904. This was probably for demonstration purposes rather than to cope with a real accident. The company also had its own ambulance section, choral society and brass band. Literature issued for customers took pride in company activities. Clarnico's was taken over by Trebor Sharps, and the Hackney works shut *c.* 1975. Trebor, merged with Bassets, now forms part of the Cadbury Group.

A TALE OF
TWO SCHOOLS

Previous pictures have touched on the long history of private schooling in Hackney. This last chapter looks at two secondary schools, Dalston County Secondary and the Grocers Company School, later Hackney Downs School. Both were transformed by changes in educational practice. Dalston County School moved sites and merged with other schools, while Hackney Downs School closed entirely in 1995.

The first view shows the main Hackney Downs School building, taken by Albert Hester, c. 1905. The school was founded by the Grocers Company, which aimed to establish a middle-class school for boys in North London. The chosen site, a triangular area south of Hackney Downs and Downs Park Road, was acquired in 1872 and the school building, designed by Theophilus Allen, was opened in September 1876.

Hackney Downs School, Lower 4b, 1913–14. The school's first headmaster was not a success and left in 1881. His successor, Revd Charles Gull, introduced major changes to the curriculum, instituted a house system and began the tradition of activity in drama and sport.

Hackney Downs School, science sixth form in the laboratory, possibly 1912–1913. Science was initially neglected at the school, though a science club existed in 1887 and went on to become one of the components of the North London Natural History Society. Gull introduced chemistry and got the Grocers Company to pay for building the laboratory. In 1907 the company transferred the school to the London County Council. Gull retired in advance of the changes and was replaced by a new headmaster, William Jenkyn Thomas, in 1905.

Hackney Downs School Battalion on parade, Hackney Downs, *c.* 1908. Gull also founded the School Battalion, which did not have uniforms so that children from homes of limited incomes would not be barred from taking part. The battalion included its own brass band and took part in shooting competitions. In the jingoistic atmosphere of the Boer War, Gull formed two Volunteer Corps, which, as the 4th London, were attached to the London Rifle Brigade and absorbed into it as E Company in 1905.

Hackney Downs School hockey team, *c.* 1895. The school had its own gymnasium, which could be converted to a swimming pool in summer. School sports included association football, cricket and annual athletics competitions. The school had a sports ground out at Edmonton after 1888, together with a house for the headmaster. The Clove Club for old boys, also founded in the Gull era in 1884, had its own range of sports and social activities.

Hackney Downs schoolboys, blowing the last post at the ceremony when the battalion stood down, 1935. Military activity seemed far less appropriate in the aftermath of the First World War. A cadet corps, formed after the Second World War, lasted until 1963. Wartime changes included evacuation to the Kings Lynn area and the repair of school buildings that had been damaged by bombing. Under the Education Act of 1944, Hackney Downs School became a county school and its governing body merged with Shacklewell Lane Secondary School in 1947.

Fire at Hackney Downs School, 18 March 1963. Members of the Fire Brigade are arriving in the aftermath of the disastrous fire. It had started in the school theatre, where a dress rehearsal for *Antigone* had finished earlier in the evening. A dimmer used to control the lighting had overheated. The blaze destroyed the theatre and the top floor, and left much of the main building unusable. New buildings replaced the old block in 1968, and in advance of their opening the school became comprehensive (though remaining for boys only) in the previous year. After a long period as a 'problem school', and following internal Hackney Council disagreement about what action to take, the school became the first in the country to be taken over by an Education Association, which closed it at the end of the autumn term of 1995.

A class at Dalston County Secondary School in the 1930s. This school had its origins as one of the Birkbeck Schools founded under the auspices of William Ellis. The Kingsland Birkbeck School opened in Colvestone Crescent in 1852, again catering for middle-class children. Board School competition from the 1870s gradually brought about its demise, and the Kingsland School was taken over by the London County Council in 1905, having had only one headmaster in its fifty-three years of existence. There were 133 pupils for the new Kingsland County Secondary School, some of whom had been fee-paying pupils at the old school, and five staff.

The obstacle race at the Dalston County Secondary School sports day, 1919. Described in the school magazine (founded in 1914) as the 'mistresses race', competitors had to eat buns suspended on strings, without using their hands. By 1910 the school had a sixth form, and improvements had been made to the laboratory and art room and a gymnasium had been built. School activities included trips to different parts of London, concerts and amateur dramatics.

Colvestone Crescent was a cramped site. After the Lady Holles School moved from Mare Street in 1934, juniors were transferred to that school's old building. In 1938 a new site on the corner of Cecelia Road was found, and the school was to have moved in the autumn of 1939, but war and evacuation intervened, and in the event pupils went to Downham Market in Norfolk and it was not until 1943 that the whole school moved to the Shacklewell site. In 1947, one pupil, Gwendoline Larner, was chosen to show Australians what a typical day was like for a British schoolgirl. Gwendoline is passing Edred House in Kings Mead Way, the council block that included her parent's flat, on route to school.

The school had its own puppet club and the thirteen-year-old Gwendoline joined in the performance.

The new Dalston County School buildings from the playground, 1947. Gwendoline is in the foreground playing tennis. Her day also included gym and art lessons. The school was renamed Dalston Mount after an amalgamation in 1974. Today, after further mergers, the school is Kingsland Comprehensive School.

After the evening meal, Gwendoline plays with her sister Audrey, before homework starts (drawing a map of Australia). Her father worked as a coal porter, having served as a military policeman in the war. His rent was 16s per week for a flat with a living room, kitchen, bathroom, toilet and three bedrooms. An elder brother and sister had already left home. Clothing was still rationed, and the full school uniform needed fourteen coupons for clothes. The two school meals cost either 5d or 6d, depending on the age of the pupil, and there was a free one-third of a pint of milk per child per day.

Joint school production of *Romeo and Juliet*, 1948. Both Hackney Downs School and Dalston County School produced their own plays, but this year the schools combined for this Shakespeare play. In the top view (Act 3, Scene 3) the Nurse (Eileen Morris) and Friar Lawrence (Pugh) are on stage with Romeo (Harold Pinter). Pinter's performance on four successive nights was described in the school magazine, which noted that he 'bore the heat and burden of the evening with unfailing vitality . . . Perhaps he excelled where strong action reinforces the words – as where he flung himself on the floor of the Friar's cell in passionate histrionic abandon.' In the bottom view the whole cast are on stage for the discovery of the body of Romeo in the last scene.

'It is my lady, oh, it is my love.' Act 2, Scene 1 from *Romeo and Juliet*, 1948. Betty Lemon played Juliet. 'Any actress who can realise for us any aspect of the essential beauty of the part deserves the gratitude of mankind', wrote the school magazine critic. All this and rejection of the 'new look' from Miss Lemon too, but it was Harold Pinter who was to go on to greater things.

INDEX